ROCKET
SCIENCE
FOR TRADERS

WILEY TRADING

Beyond Candlesticks/Steve Nison
Beyond Technical Analysis, Second Edition/Tushar Chande
Contrary Opinion/R. Earl Hadady
Cybernetic Trading Strategies/Murray A. Ruggiero, Jr.
Encyclopedia of Chart Patterns/Thomas Bulkowski
Expert Trading Systems/John R. Wolberg
Four Steps to Trading Success/John F. Clayburg
Fundamental Analysis/Jack Schwager
Gaming the Market/Ronald B. Shelton
Genetic Algorithms and Investment Strategies/Richard J. Bauer, Jr.
Intermarket Technical Analysis/John J. Murphy
Long-Term Secrets to Short-Term Trading/Larry Williams
Macro Trading and Investment Strategies/Gabriel Burstein
Managed Trading/Jack Schwager
McMillan on Options/Lawrence G. McMillan
Neural Network Time Series Forecasting of Financial Markets/E. Michael Azoff
New Market Timing Techniques/Thomas R. DeMark
Nonlinear Pricing/Christopher T. May
Option Market Making/Alan J. Baird
Option Strategies, Second Edition/Courtney Smith
Pattern, Price & Time/James A. Hyerczyk
Point and Figure Charting/Thomas J. Dorsey
Profits from Natural Resources/Roland A. Jansen
Rocket Science for Traders: Digital Signal Processing Applications/John F. Ehlers
Schwager on Futures/Jack Schwager
Seasonality/Jake Bernstein
Stock Index Futures & Options/Susan Abbott Gidel
Study Guide for Trading for a Living/Dr. Alexander Elder
Study Guide to Accompany Fundamental Analysis/Jack Schwager
Study Guide to Accompany Technical Analysis/Jack Schwager
Technical Analysis/Jack Schwager
Technical Analysis of the Options Markets/Richard Hexton
Technical Market Indicators/Richard J. Bauer, Jr., and Julie R. Dahlquist
The Day Trader's Manual/William F. Eng
The Dynamic Option Selection System/Howard L. Simons
The Hedge Fund Edge/Mark Boucher
The Intuitive Trader/Robert Koppel
The Mathematics of Money Management/Ralph Vince
The New Market Wizards/Jack Schwager
The New Money Management/Ralph Vince
The New Options Market, Fourth Edition/Max Ansbacher
The New Science of Technical Analysis/Thomas R. DeMark
The New Technical Trader/Tushar Chande and Stanley S. Kroll
The Option Advisor/Bernie G. Schaeffer
The Options Course/George A. Fontanills
The Options Course Workbook/George A. Fontanills
The Trader's Tax Survival Guide, Revised Edition/Ted Tesser
The Trader's Tax Solution/Ted Tesser
The Trading Game/Ryan Jones
The Ultimate Trading Guide/John Hill, George Pruitt, Lundy Hill
The Visual Investor/John J. Murphy
Trader Vic II/Victor Sperandeo
Trading Applications of Japanese Candlestick Charting/Gary Wagner and Brad Matheny
Trading Chaos/Bill Williams
Trading for a Living/Dr. Alexander Elder
Trading Systems & Methods, Third Edition/Perry Kaufman
Trading the Plan/Robert Deel
Trading to Win/Ari Kiev
Trading with Crowd Psychology/Carl Gyllenram
Trading without Fear/Richard W. Arms, Jr.

ROCKET SCIENCE FOR TRADERS

Digital Signal Processing Applications

John F. Ehlers

John Wiley & Sons, Inc.

New York • Chichester • Weinheim • Brisbane • Singapore • Toronto

Published by John Wiley & Sons, Inc.
Published simultaneously in Canada.

Library of Congress Cataloging-in-Publication Data:

Ehlers, John F.
    Rocket science for traders : digital signal processing applications / John F. Ehlers.
       p. cm.—(Wiley trading)
     ISBN 0-471-40567-1 (cloth : alk. paper)
      1. Investment analysis—Mathematical models.   2. Stocks—Prices—Mathematical models.   3. Signal processing—Digital techniques.   I. Title.   II. Series.

HG4529 .E49 2001
332.63'2042'01154—dc21   2001017853

10 9 8 7 6 5 4 3

To Elizabeth—my friend, my companion, my wife.

PREFACE: LIFT OFF

*Any sufficiently advanced technology is
indistinguishable from magic.*

—SIR ARTHUR C. CLARKE

The advances made in computer technology during the past two
decades have been dramatic. The computer power to which we
have access today is far greater and more powerful than that
which was available to the entire national defense system just
30 years ago. Software for traders, however, has not kept pace.
Most of the trading tools available today are neither different nor
more complex than the simple pencil-and-paper calculations
that can be achieved through the use of mechanical adding
machines. True, these calculations are now made with blinding
speed and presented in colorful and eye-grabbing displays, but
the power and usefulness of these procedures have not changed.
If anything, the relative power of the calculations has dimin-
ished because the increased speed of information exchange
and increased market capitalization have caused fundamental
shifts in the technical character of the market. These shifts
include increased volatility and shorter periods for the market
swings.

Rocket Science for Traders promises to revolutionize the art
of trading by introducing modern digital signal processing to the
playing field. The application of digital signal processing offers

the advantage of viewing old problems from a new perspective. The new perspective gained by digital signal processing has led to the birth and development of some profoundly effective new trading tools. The advances in new trading tools, along with the continuing advancements in hardware capabilities, virtually ensure the continued application of digital signal processing in the future. The trader who masters the fundamental concepts of digital signal processing, therefore, will find great advantage when approaching the volatile market of the twenty-first century.

A brief introductory chapter is followed by Chapter 2, in which the philosophical bases for Trend Modes and Cycle Modes are established through a look at solutions to a constrained version of the Random Walk problem. Specific indicators that target each of these modes are developed later in the book. Chapters 3 and 4 include observations about conventional technical analysis tools, with special attention given to some of their common pitfalls.

The basis of efficient digital signal processing is the use of complex arithmetic for all computations. Since complex variables are often completely foreign to most traders, a brief review and introduction to phasors are provided in Chapter 5. The common waveforms with which everyone is familiar are called analytic waveforms. These are converted into complex variables using the Hilbert Transform, as described in Chapter 6. The ability of the Hilbert Transform to meet the requirements of traders means little if the system is not used alongside a measurement of the market cycle. Several different algorithms for cycle measurement are therefore described and compared in Chapter 7.

The Homodyne Discriminator proves itself to be the preferred algorithm and is thus used throughout the remainder of the book. Chapters 8 through 12 develop unique indicators from the complex variable waveforms. These include the Signal-to-Noise Ratio (which indicates when trading should be avoided), the Sinewave Indicator (which anticipates Cycle Mode turning points without creating false whipsaw signals in the Trend Mode), an Instantaneous Trendline, and the logic to automatically ascertain the current trading mode of the market. These concepts are then combined to form a profitable automatic trading system.

The use of digital signal processing for trading almost always involves the employment of filters. Digital filter transfer responses are most efficiently described using Z Transforms, which are described in Chapter 13. The most common Finite Impulse Response (FIR) and Infinite Impulse Response (IIR) filters are described in Chapters 14 and 15, including equations to compute filters on the fly, as well as tabulated coefficients for more static applications. More specialized filters are described in the following chapters. These include smoothing filters that have the lag removed (Chapter 16) and a unique MESA Adaptive Moving Average (MAMA) (Chapter 17). We introduce the Ehlers filter, one of the most flexible nonlinear filters available, and one that has the potential to be a true market model (Chapter 18).

The use of Fast Fourier Transforms (FFT) is often advocated by those who ignore mathematical constraints as a way to measure the market spectra. Chapter 19 is dedicated to explaining why traders should avoid FFTs in market analysis. This chapter alone will save the reader money by illustrating that FFTs are inappropriate tools for trading. Novel and unique concepts are presented in the following chapters. The theoretically optimum predictive filter is described and defined in terms of the phasor diagram.

This concept produces a moving average with no lag and thus has an ability to generate trading signals that are very close to each turning point in the market. When filtering alone is inadequate to isolate the signals from the noise, unique displays enable visual interpretation that is well outside the bandwidth of electronic filters. The procedure to plot the signal phasor is provided for just this purpose.

Rocket Science for Traders concludes with approaches to make conventional indicators, such as the RSI, Stochastic, and CCI, adaptive to current market conditions rather than using static parameters. Specific methods are given for these indicators. Additionally, the general concepts presented for these can be extended to apply to any existing static indicator.

Many of the digital signal processing techniques described in this book have been known for many years and used in the physical sciences. The Maximum Entropy Spectral Analysis (MESA) algorithm was originally developed by geophysicists in their exploration for oil. The small amount of data from seismic exploration demanded a solution using a short amount of data. I successfully adapted this approach and popularized it for the measurement of market cycles. More recently, the use of digital signal processing has exploded in consumer electronics, making devices such as CDs and DVDs possible. Today, complete radio receivers are constructed without the use of analog components. As we expand its use by introducing it to the field of trading, we see that digital signal processing is an exciting new field, perfect for technically oriented traders. It allows us to generalize and expand the use of many traditional indicators, as well as achieve more precise computations. My objective is to expose you to these techniques to make your trading more profitable and more pleasurable.

Traders who have never studied mathematics or who have let their math skills languish may find some of the concepts presented to be foreign and difficult to grasp at the first reading. Since many of the concepts are interrelated, a deeper understanding may come from rereading this book several times.

JOHN F. EHLERS

Santa Barbara, California
June 2001

ACKNOWLEDGMENTS

I would like to acknowledge the impact that Dr. Carl Jelinek had on my approach, resulting from our many technical discussions. Dr. Jelinek has enabled me to better understand how the dynamics of the probability density function of market prices profoundly affect our trading modes. As a result, I have attempted to implement approaches that best capture profitable trading conditions. I would also like to acknowledge the contributions of Donald H. Kraska, whose rigorous attention to detail kept me honest in some of my more arm-waving derivations. Most of all, I would like to acknowledge the support of my customers who made my research possible and for the encouragement of my colleagues.

J. F. E.

CONTENTS

Chapter 1   Introduction to the Science of Digital
               Signal Analysis   1

Chapter 2   Market Modes   9

Chapter 3   Moving Averages   17

Chapter 4   Momentum Functions   33

Chapter 5   Complex Variables   41

Chapter 6   Hilbert Transforms   51

Chapter 7   Measuring Cycle Periods   63

Chapter 8   Signal-to-Noise Ratio   79

Chapter 9   The Sinewave Indicator   95

Chapter 10   The Instantaneous Trendline   107

Chapter 11   Identifying Market Modes   113

Chapter 12   Designing a Profitable Trading System   119

Chapter 13   Transform Arithmetic   131

Chapter 14   Finite Impulse Response Filters   143

Chapter 15   Infinite Impulse Response Filters   151

Chapter 16   Removing Lag   167

Contents

Chapter 17   MAMA—The Mother of Adaptive
              Moving Averages   177

Chapter 18   Ehlers Filters   185

Chapter 19   Measuring Market Spectra   197

Chapter 20   Optimum Predictive Filters   205

Chapter 21   What You See Is What You Get   215

Chapter 22   Making Standard Indicators Adaptive   227

              Epilogue   239

              For More Information   240

              Glossary   241

              Index   245

Chapter 1

INTRODUCTION TO
THE SCIENCE OF
DIGITAL SIGNAL ANALYSIS

Computers are worthless.
They can only give you answers.

—PABLO PICASSO

Make no mistake about it. This is a book for traders about digital signal processing. It is not a book for engineers about trading. At first glance, the reverse may seem to be true for many traders because the subject matter is on the cutting edge of technology and the mathematics behind this technology can be more advanced than that encountered in school. Recognizing that many traders want to simply use the technology rather than become schooled in it, the information in this book is aimed at several levels. We provide the rationale, derive the equations, and provide the computer code to implement the techniques. With this approach, our results can be used in applications ranging from a cookie-cutter indicator operating within TradeStation or Super-Charts to the applications that are springboards for still more advanced technology.

It is common for technical analysis indicators to be described in terms of a fixed period of time. For example, the standard length used for a Relative Strength Indicator (RSI) is the last 14 price bars. One often hears about a five-day Stochastic or a 10/30-day moving average system. Since the market is continuously changing, there is absolutely no reason to use static periods in your indicators. Choosing the correct time period is essential to using traditional indicators to their maximum potential. While deriving the tools with which to make indicators adaptive, you will see novel indicators that surpass the traditional ones in accuracy and performance.

Digital signal processing is an exciting new field for technically oriented traders. Many of the indicators that have been used previously can now be generalized, and the computations can now be accomplished more precisely using digital methods. It is interesting to note that many of the digital signal processing techniques I describe have been known for many years and used in the physical sciences. My objective is to expose you to these techniques to make your trading more profitable and more pleasurable.

Many physical systems involve the use of analog signals that are represented as continuous time functions. There is an amplitude associated with the signal at each instant in time. There is an infinite number of amplitude values that the signal may assume. However, if the signal is frequency bandlimited, there is no significant energy above the cutoff frequency. Since energy is required in any physical system to change amplitude, this implies that the signal cannot change amplitude instantaneously. Therefore, points closely spaced in time will have relatively similar amplitudes. There are several ways in which a signal can be represented other than as a continuous analog signal. One method is to quantize the amplitude and hold that value until the next quantization is performed. There are a finite number of amplitudes, but the function is continuous in time. This is in contrast to a discrete time signal, which has continuous amplitude values but is only defined at discrete instants in time. As with analog signals, there is an infinite number of levels, but there are only a finite number of points in time. If a signal is quantized in both amplitude and time, it is called a *digital signal*. The data we deal with in trading are digital signals from sampling that is done in uniform periods of time (once per day, once per hour, etc.).

A discrete time signal can be obtained from an analog signal by multiplying it by a periodic impulse train. The sampling signal can be expressed in the time domain as

$$s(t) = \sum_{k = -\infty}^{\infty} \delta(t - kT)$$

where δ = the impulse function
         T = period between impulses

Using Fourier theory, multiplication in the frequency domain is synonymous with convolution in the time domain. In other words, multiplying signals in the time domain is the same as *heterodyning*, or mixing, the signals in the frequency domain. The impulse train has an infinite number of harmonics at frequencies that are the reciprocal of the period between pulses.

The effects of sampling in the frequency domain are illustrated in Figure 1.1. The continuous bandlimited signal $F(f)$ is shown in the top segment (a) as having a frequency rolloff at some point. In the middle segment (b), the sampling impulse waveform $S(f)$ has a monochromatic spectral line at the sampling frequency f_s and all its harmonics. When the sampling is performed on the bandlimited signal, the convolved waveform is shown in the bottom segment (c). Not only is the original bandlimited continuous signal present, but this same signal also appears as the upper and lower sidebands of each sampling frequency harmonic. Since the lower sideband of the sampling frequency can extend into the original baseband, the bandlimiting must occur below half the sampling frequency. Half the sampling frequency is called the *Nyquist frequency* because the Nyquist Sampling Theorem states that there must be at least two samples per cycle of the signal to avoid aliasing.

Aliasing is a form of distortion. It results from sampling a continuous signal less than twice per cycle. This distortion can be seen in the two waveforms depicted in Figure 1.2. Both the upper trace and the lower trace have identical sampling points, denoted by the dots. The samples in the top trace appear to be valid. However, these same samples plot out the sine wave of the lower trace, where there are four samples per cycle. The dif-

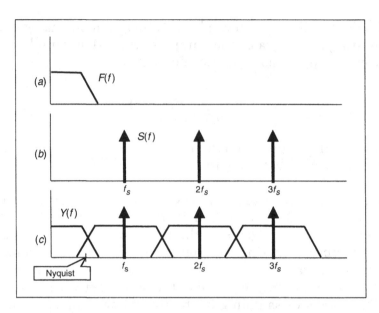

Figure 1.1.   Sampled data in the frequency domain.

ference is explained by aliasing in the top trace. The samples are taken at three-quarters of a cycle apart, or two samples every one-and-a-half cycles. This does not meet the Nyquist criterion of at least two samples per cycle.

In trading, we can scale all time frames to each bar. Each bar is a sample. Therefore, to meet the Nyquist criterion, the absolute shortest cycle we can consider is a 2-bar cycle. As a practical matter, 5- and 6-bar cycles should be considered the shortest useful cycles.

If the input signal is insufficiently bandlimited, the aliased frequency components are folded back into the sampled baseband as false signals and noise. For this reason, data should always be smoothed before any other operation is performed. Otherwise, the undesired signal components will have an adverse effect on your computations. Smoothing removes the high-frequency components, precluding these components from being folded back into the analysis bandwidth.

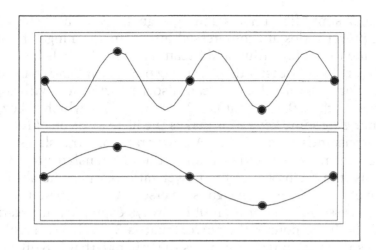

Figure 1.2.   Signals must be sampled at least twice per cycle.

The complex waveshapes that describe traders' charts can be considered as synthesized from more primitive waveshapes, adding or subtracting from each other depending on their relative phases. These kinds of waves are called *coherent*, meaning the amplitude at any given position can be determined by a vector addition of the amplitudes. The waveshapes are analogous to voltage in electric circuits. When we measure the strength of the signals, we prefer not to use the amplitude of the wave as a measure because it is dependent on the location, or phase, within the wave. Rather, power is the preferred measure of strength. Power is proportional to waveform amplitude squared, just as the power a 100-W lightbulb consumes from a 115-V circuit is proportional to the voltage squared. In digital signal analysis, we are mostly concerned with relative power, or power ratios. It is convenient to express these power ratios in terms of decibels.

As an historical aside, one decibel was the power lost in a telephone signal over one mile of wire (the name was derived from Alexander Graham Bell). A decibel is one-tenth of a bel. The bel is the logarithm base 10 of the power ratio. Thus, a decibel is $10*Log_{10}(P2/P1)$, and is abbreviated as dB. Working with

decibels simplifies understanding signal levels both because
large power ratios are compressed into a smaller range of numbers due to the logarithm and because adding decibels (i.e., adding logarithms) is easier than carrying out multiplication in your
head. For example, $2*2 = 4$ can also be performed with logarithms: $Log(2) = 0.3$, so that $Log(2) + Log(2) = 0.6$, which is $Log(4)$.
Memorizing some key ratios makes the identification of relative
power instantly recognizable. A power ratio of 2 translates to +3
dB. If that ratio is ½ rather than 2, then it translates to –3 dB.
That is, the reciprocal of the power ratio is the same absolute
value of decibels, but the sign is reversed. A ratio smaller than 1
(but necessarily greater than 0) is always expressed in negative
decibels. If we double the power, that is 3 dB. If we double it
again so that the power is 4 times the original, that is 6 dB. Doubling still again to get 8 times the original power, we add another
3 dB to reach a level of 9 dB. Since we have a logarithm base 10,
a power ratio of 10 is 10 dB, and a power ratio of 100 is 20 dB, and
so on. Consider this to further illustrate the use of decibel: If a
filter has half the power coming out of it as was entered, the output power is –3 dB. The filter is said to have a 3-dB loss. If a similar filter is placed at the output of the first, the net output power
from the composite circuit would be –6 dB.

The measurement –3 dB is usually a critical point for a filter.
This half-power point in the filter response occurs when the
wave amplitude is 0.7 relative to its maximum value. This is true
because $0.7*0.7 = 0.5$, the half-power ratio. The critical point in
the filter is often called the *cutoff frequency* because frequency
components beyond the cutoff frequency are attenuated to a
greater degree and frequency components within the cutoff frequency are attenuated very little. To simplify, think of the filter
as having a stone-wall response. In this analogy, frequencies
below the cutoff frequency are not attenuated and frequencies
above the cutoff frequency are not allowed to pass through the
filter.

EasyLanguage is currently the most popular computer language for traders. Thus, I use this system to generate computer
codes. EasyLanguage is a dialect of Pascal, containing specialized keywords unique to trading. Because it reads almost like

English, EasyLanguage is almost effortless to understand. It is also easy to translate to other computer languages. When translating, the reference convention must be understood. The Easy-Language assumption is that all computations are done with reference to the current bar. For example, Close means the closing price of the current bar. If there is a reference associated with that parameter, it is displayed in square brackets and means the number of bars back to which it refers. For example, Close[3] refers to the closing price 3 bars ago. Zero can be used as a reference, and has the same meaning as the current bar without any reference (there is no reference into the future). As a further example, a two-day momentum is written as Momentum = Close – Close[2];. Each completed line of code must terminate in a semicolon. For clarity, I always write out the generic description of an action rather than relying on a more esoteric Trade-Station function call. As a result, the computer code presented should be easily translated to BASIC, C++, or even an Excel spreadsheet.

Key Points to Remember

- This book can be read at several levels, ranging from a broad perspective overview to detailed computer coding.
- Novel and unique indicators are made possible by the mathematical techniques to be introduced.
- Even conventional indicator performance can be enhanced by making them adaptive to current market conditions.
- Time scales of financial data can be dealt with on a per-bar basis. The absolute time scale of the data is irrelevant for computational purposes.
- Working with sampled data is distinctly different from working with continuous information. Sampled data should always be smoothed to avoid erratic signals.

Chapter 2

MARKET MODES

Chaos often breeds life, when order breeds habit.

—HENRY BROOKS ADAMS

The whole point of technical analysis is to find a way to exploit the inefficiency of the market for gain. The general objective of the market is to provide accurate prices for asset allocation. That is, investors can choose strategies that allow prices to fully reflect all available information at any time. Such a market (a market in which prices always fully reflect available information) is called efficient. Much research has been done to prove that the market is indeed efficient. However, the fact that there exists a number of traders who are continuously successful is adequate proof that markets are not necessarily completely efficient. The failure of the efficiency hypothesis in several cases is sufficient evidence to invalidate the hypothesis itself.

Classical efficient market models are often concerned with the adjustment of security prices to three information subsets. Weak form tests comprise the first subset, in which we are simply given the historical prices. The second subset is semistrong form tests that concern themselves with whether prices efficiently adjust to other publicly available information. Strong form tests, the third subset, are concerned with whether investors have monopolistic access to any information relevant to price formation. The general conclusion, particularly for the weak form tests, is that the markets can be only marginally profitable to a trader. In fact, only the strong form tests are viewed as benchmarks against deviations from market efficiency. These strong form tests point to activities such as insider trading and the market-making function of specialists.

The efficient-markets-model statement that the price fully reflects available information implies that successive price changes are independent of one another. In addition, it has usually been assumed that successive changes are identically distributed. Together, these two hypotheses constitute the *Random Walk Model,* which says that the conditional and marginal probability distributions of an independent random variable are identical. In addition, it says that the probability density function must be the same for all time. This model is clearly flawed. If the mean return is constant over time, then the return is independent of any information available at a given time.

I assume that there is an adequate number of traders involved in making the market that a statistical analysis involving a Random Walk is appropriate. There must be several constraints to such a Random Walk. The first constraint is that the prices be constrained to one dimension—they can only go up or down. The second constraint is that time must progress monotonically.

I have formed my philosophical basis of market action from extensive work using constrained Random Walks in the physical sciences.[1] The expression of such a Random Walk is that of a drunkard moving on a one-dimensional array of regularly spaced points. At regular intervals, the drunkard flips a coin and makes one step to the right or left, depending on the outcome of the coin toss. At the end of n steps, he can be at any one of $2n + 1$ sites, and the probability that he is at any site can be calculated. Let the distance between the points on the lattice be ΔL, and let the time between successive steps be ΔT. If ΔL and ΔT are allowed to shrink to zero in such a way that $(\Delta L)^2/\Delta T$ remains constant to the diffusion constant D, then the equation governing the distribution of the displacement of the Random Walker from his starting point is

[1]Weiss, G. H., and R. J. Rubin. "Random Walks: Theory and Selected Applications." *Advances in Chemical Physics* 52 (1982): 363–505.

$$\frac{\delta P}{\delta t} = D\frac{\delta^2 P}{\delta x^2}$$

This rather famous partial differential equation is called the *Diffusion Equation*. The function $P(x,t)$ can be interpreted in two ways. It can either be taken to express the probability density or the concentration of diffusing matter at position x at time t. Following the latter interpretation, it can, for example, describe the way heat flows up the stem of a silver spoon when placed in a hot cup of coffee.

To better understand the theory of diffusion, imagine the way a smoke plume leaves a smokestack. Think about how the smoke rises compared to how a trend carries itself through the market. A gentle breeze determines the angle to which the smoke, or trend, is bent. The widening of the smoke plume represents the probability density of the smoke particles as a function of distance from the smokestack. This widening is analogous to the decreased accuracy of the prediction of future trend prices further into the future.

The formulation of the Drunkard's Walk has no property that can be regarded as the analog of momentum. A more realistic model of a physical object's motion needs to account for some form of memory—we need to know where the object came from and the likelihood it will continue to move in the same direction. The simplest modification of the Random Walk is to allow the coin toss to determine the persistence of motion. In other words, with probability p the drunkard makes his next step in the same direction as the last one, and with probability $1-p$ he makes a move in the opposite direction. The ordinary Drunkard's Walk occurs when $p = \frac{1}{2}$, because either move is equally likely. The interesting feature of the modified Drunkard's Walk is that as the distance between the point and the time between steps decreases, one no longer obtains the Diffusion Equation, but rather the following equation:

$$\frac{\delta^2 P}{\delta t^2} + \frac{1}{T}\frac{\delta P}{\delta t} = c^2\frac{\delta^2 P}{\delta x^2}$$

in one dimension, where T and c^2 are constants. This is another famous partial differential equation called the *Telegrapher's*

Equation. This equation expresses the idea that diffusion occurs in restricted regions, such that $x^2 < c^2t^2$. That is, the position must be less than the velocity of propagation c multiplied by time t. More important, the Telegrapher's Equation describes the harmonic motion of $P(x,t)$ just as surely as it describes the electric wave traveling down a pair of wires.

Harmonic motion is ubiquitous. It is the natural response to a disturbance on any scale ranging from the atomic to the galactic. You can demonstrate the effect by holding a ruler over the edge of a table, bending the ruler down, and then releasing it. The resulting vibration is harmonic motion. Alternatively, you can stretch a rubber band between your fingers, pull the band to one side, and then release it. The oscillations of the rubber band also constitute harmonic motion. Since there are plenty of opportunities for market disturbances, it is only a small stretch to extend the solution to the Drunkard's Walk problem from physical phenomena and use it to describe the action of the market.

The Drunkard's Walk solution can describe two market conditions. In the first condition, the probability is evenly divided between stepping to the right or the left, resulting in the *Trend Mode*, which is described by the Diffusion Equation. The second condition, the probability of motion direction is skewed, results in the *Cycle Mode*, which is described by the Telegrapher's Equation. The difference between the two conditions can be as simple as the question that the majority of traders constantly ask themselves. If the question is "I wonder if the market will go up or down?" then the probability of market movement is about 50-50, establishing the conditions for a Trend Mode. However, if the question is posed as "Will the trend continue?" then the conditions are such that the Telegrapher's Equation applies. As a result, the Cycle Mode of the market can be established.

The Telegrapher's Equation solution also describes the meandering of a river. Viewed as an aerial photograph, every river in the world meanders. This meandering is not due to a lack of homogeneity in the soil, but to the conservation of energy. (You can appreciate that soil homogeneity is not a factor because other streams, such as ocean currents, also meander in a nearly homogeneous medium.) Ocean currents are not nearly as visible as rivers and are, therefore, not as familiar to most of us. Every meander in a river is independent of other meanders, and are all thus completely random. If we were to look at all the meanders as an ensemble, overlaying one on top of the other like a multiple exposure photograph, the meander randomness would also become apparent. The composite envelope of the river paths would be about the same as the cross section of the smoke plume. However, if we are in a given meander, we are virtually certain of the general path of the river for a short distance downstream. The result is that the river can be described as having a short-term coherency but a randomness over the longer span.

River meanders are like the cycles we have in the market. We can measure and use these short-term cycles to our advantage if we realize they can come and go in the longer term.

We can extend our analogy to understand when short-term cycles occur. Rivers meander in an attempt to maintain a constant slope on their way to the ocean. If the slope is too severe, the meander has the same effect as a skier who weaves back and forth across a slope to slow the descent. The flow of a river physically adjusts itself for the purpose of energy conservation. If the water speeds up, the width of the river decreases to yield a constant flow volume. The faster flow contains more kinetic energy, and the river attempts to slow it down by changing direction. At the same time, the river direction cannot change abruptly because of the momentum of the water's flow. Meandering results. Thus, meanders cause the river to take the path of least resistance in the sense of energy conservation. We should think of markets in the same way. Time must progress as surely as the river must flow to the ocean. Overbought and oversold conditions result from attempts to conserve the energy of the market. This particular energy arises from the fear and greed of traders.

Again, it may be useful to test the principle of energy conservation for yourself. Tear a strip about 1 inch wide along the side of a standard sheet of paper about 11 inches long. Grasp each end of this strip between the thumb and forefinger of each hand. Now move your hands toward one another. Your compression is putting energy into this strip, and its natural response can take one of four modes. These modes are determined by the boundary conditions that you force. If both hands are pointing up, the response is a single upward arc, approximating one alternation of a sine wave. If both hands are pointing down, the response is a downward arc. If either hand is pointing up and the other pointing down, the strip response to the energy input is approximately a full sine wave. These four lowest modes are the natural responses following the principle of conservation of energy. You can introduce additional bends in the strip, but a minor jiggling will cause the paper to snap to one of the four lowest modes, with the exact mode depending on the boundary conditions that you impose. The two full sinewave modes are approximately the second harmonic of the two single alternation modes.

The market only has a single dominant cycle most of the time. When multiple cycles are simultaneously present, they are generally harmonically related. This is not to say that nonharmonic simultaneous cycles cannot exist—just that they are rare enough to be discounted in simplified models of market action. The general observation of a single dominant cycle tends to support the notion that the natural response to a disturbance is monotonic harmonic motion.

It is true that if you are a hammer, the rest of the world looks like a nail. We must take care to recognize that all market action is not strictly described by cycles alone and that cycle tools are not always appropriate. A more complete model of the market can be achieved by knowing that there are times when the solution to the Telegrapher's Equation prevails and times when the solution to the Diffusion Equation applies. We can, therefore, divide the market action into a Cycle Mode and a Trend Mode. By having only two modes in our market model, we can switch our trading strategy back and forth between them, using the more appropriate tool according to our situation. Since our digital signal processing tools analyze cycles, we can establish that a Trend Mode is more appropriate at any given time due to the failure of a Cycle Mode.

There are many ways to analyze the market using technical analysis. Regarding indicators, the preferred tools are moving averages or data smoothers for Trend Modes and oscillator-type indicators for Cycle Modes. In later chapters, we develop superior indicators for both market modes. At this point, it is important to understand that the two modes of a simplified market model have been directly derived from solutions to the Drunkard's Walk problem. Keep asking yourself, "Will the market go up or down today?" and "I wonder if the trend will continue?"

Key Points to Remember

- A simplified model of the market has a Trend Mode and a Cycle Mode.
- The market model is similar to a meandering river.
- Both the Trend Mode and the Cycle Mode are derived from the Drunkard's Walk.
- Different technical indicators are appropriate for each market mode.

Chapter 3

MOVING AVERAGES

Trend is not destiny.

—Lewis Mumford

Centuries ago Karl Friedrich Gauss proved that the average is the best estimator of the random variable. He derived the familiar bell-shaped probability density curve known as the *Gaussian*, or Normal, *distribution*. When the probability distribution of a random variable is unknown, the Gaussian distribution is generally assumed. In this bell-shaped curve, the peak value, or the mean, is the nominal forecast. The width of the variation from the mean is described in terms of the variance. It is certainly true that the average is the best estimator for the market in the case where the Diffusion Equation (as described in Chapter 2) applies. The best estimate of the location of any smoke particle is the average across the width of the plume. This is probably why moving averages are heavily used by technical traders—they want the best estimate of the random variable.

All moving averages have two characteristics in common: They smooth the data and cause lag because they depend on historical information for computation. By far the most serious implication for traders is the induced lag. Lag delays any buying or selling decision and is almost always a bad characteristic. Therefore, averaging is typically a trade-off between the amount of desired smoothing and the amount of lag that can be tolerated.

There are three popular types of moving averages. These are

1. Simple Moving Average (SMA)
2. Weighted Moving Average (WMA)
3. Exponential Moving Average (EMA)

Each of these types of averages has its own respective merit, and there are times when any one of the three is the appropriate choice. The discussions in this chapter describe each of the three moving averages so you can make the comparisons for your own applications.

Simple Moving Average

An n-day simple average is formed by adding the prices of a security over n days and dividing by n. Thus, the weighted price for each day is the real price divided by n. The simple average becomes a moving average by adding the next day's weighted price to the sum and dropping off the weighted first day's price. Thus, the simple average moves from day to day. This is the most efficient way to compute a Simple Moving Average (SMA). Another way to view an SMA is as an average of the data within a window. In this concept, the window slides across the chart, forming the moving average from bar to bar, as shown in Figure 3.1. Figure 3.1 shows a 10-bar window and the moving average formed by this window. The average is plotted at the right-hand side of the window, causing the moving average lag. This is necessary because the window cannot accept data into the future. So, when a moving average is used in actual trading, the lag cannot be overcome. Centering the moving average on the window is not helpful for trading because future data would be required to get the current value of the average. Obviously, future data are not available for the last bar on the chart. The static lag of an SMA can be computed as a function of the window width. Consider the following case where the data have a price of zero at the left edge of the window. The price increases by one unit for each subsequent bar, as shown in Figure 3.2. The average price is always the price at the center of the window, expressed mathematically at $(n - 1)/2$. The average is

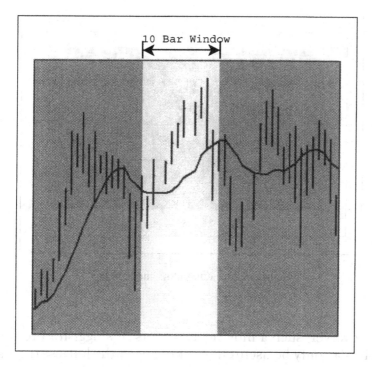

Figure 3.1. A moving average averages data within a moving window.

Chart created with TradeStation2000i® by Omega Research, Inc.

plotted at the right-hand side of the window. Since the price slope is unity (rises vertically one unit for each unit increase along the horizontal), the averaged price at the right-hand side of the window is effectively lagging the price at the center of the window by $(n - 1)/2$ bars. This lag is simply unavoidable. An example of a 5-bar window average is shown in Figure 3.2. It is clear in this example that the lag is two units, equal to $(5 - 1)/2$. As a trader, you must make a trade-off by choosing between the amount of smoothing you want from your moving average and the amount of lag you can tolerate.

A thorough understanding of the impact of moving average lag is absolutely crucial for successful trading. On the one hand, a wide averaging window provides a very smooth moving aver-

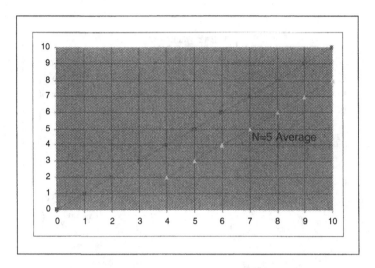

Figure 3.2. Computing the SMA lag.

age. However, such a moving average is so sluggish in response
that it may only be useful in working with the longest trends. A
narrow averaging window, on the other hand, does not provide
much smoothing, so the average may be highly responsive but
can produce whipsaw signals due to inadequate smoothing.
Approaching a moving average from the perspective of the frequency domain rather than from the time domain can thus be
useful and instructive.

Assume the data comprise a theoretical sine wave as shown
in Figure 3.3. We can arrange our averaging window to be any
width we choose. The width of Window A in Figure 3.3 is
exactly one half cycle. If the window were narrower, then the
average would not include all the data points in the positive
alternation of the sine wave, and the average would therefore be
less sensitive. If the window were wider than a half cycle, the
average would contain some negative data points as well as all
the data points in the positive alternation. Thus, the average
would also be less sensitive. Figure 3.3 shows the half-period
moving average of a sine wave. The peak value of this moving
average occurs at the right-hand side of Window A because Win-

dow A contains only the positive data points in the sine wave. As we move the window to the right, the moving average decreases in amplitude. Reaching Window B, the moving average is zero at the right-hand edge because Window B contains exactly as many negative data points as positive data points, causing the average to sum to zero. Continuing to move the window to the right, we arrive at Window C. The moving average at Window C is maximum negative because Window C contains only negative data points. The moving average is created by sliding the window across the entire data set.

Note that the half-period SMA of a sine wave is another sinusoid (waves that look like sine waves), delayed by a quarter cycle. Drawing from our previous knowledge of the lag of an SMA, we can assert that the lag is half the window width, expressed in fractions of a cycle period or in degrees of phase. A quarter-cycle SMA will lag the price by an eighth of a cycle. This is the equivalent of saying that if the averaging window is 90 degrees wide, the resulting SMA lag will be 45 degrees.

When the market is in a Cycle Mode, it is more important to think in terms of the phase shift an SMA will induce rather than in terms of the number of bars of lag that it will cause. For example, a 2-bar lag is almost inconsequential for a 40-bar cycle.

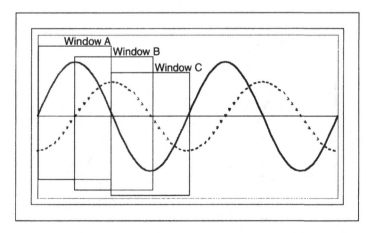

Figure 3.3. Half-cycle SMA of a sine wave.

However, this same 2-bar lag is a full quarter-of-a-cycle phase shift for an 8-bar cycle. In trading, it is important to always consider the phases in relative terms, particularly when dealing with shorter cycles. For this reason, it is often preferable to continuously adapt an SMA window to be a fraction of the measured market cycle rather than using a fixed window width. This adaptation enables the SMA to provide the same reaction to price movement regardless of the time period of the dominant cycle.

If we increase the window width to include a full cycle, as shown in Figure 3.4, we have a very interesting case for the SMA. Examination of Figure 3.4 shows that in a pure cycle, when the window width is exactly one cycle, there are as many data points above the mean as there are below it. Therefore, the SMA is exactly zero for this special case. We use this phenomenon later to create the Instantaneous Trendline after we have measured the dominant cycle. By adjusting the average to have a window whose width is exactly the measured dominant cycle, we cancel out the dominant cycle completely. Since our simplified market model consists of a Trend Mode component and a Cycle Mode component, we are left with only the Trend Mode component after the dominant cycle component has been re-

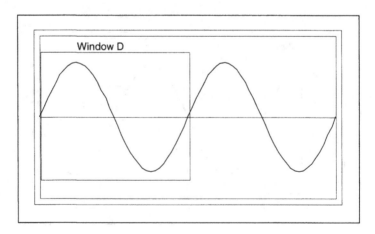

Figure 3.4.   The average of a full-cycle SMA is zero.

moved. The Instantaneous Trendline differs from an SMA only in the respect that the window width can vary from bar to bar. Since the window width is always a full cycle period for this indicator, the lag of the Instantaneous Trendline is a half period of the dominant cycle.

The SMA is also identically zero for a pure sine wave when the window width is exactly an integer number of cycles wide. This can be seen in Figure 3.5, in which the window width is 12 bars. Figure 3.5 is attained by changing the frequency applied to the fixed 12-bar-wide window. The results are plotted after being normalized to the Nyquist frequency, which is exactly half the sampling frequency. For example, if the data being used consist of daily bars, then the Nyquist frequency is 0.5 bars per day. Since the cycle period and the cycle frequency are inversely proportional, the period of the Nyquist frequency is 2 bars. The periods of those components that have an integer number of cycles within the 12-bar window have been noted in Figure 3.5.

The SMA window can be viewed as a transfer function that multiplies the data falling within the window by 1 and multiplies all data outside the window by 0. This transfer response is a pulse in the time domain. Functions in the time domain are related to functions in the frequency domain by the Fourier Transform, as discussed in Chapter 1. A derivation of Fourier Transforms is beyond the scope of this book, but is covered in

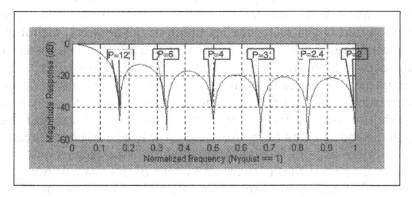

Figure 3.5. The transfer response of a 12-bar SMA.

many fine texts. Without the derivation, I assert that the Fourier Transform of the pulse in the time domain is

$$SMA(Period) = Sin(\pi * W/P)/(\pi * W/P)$$

where W = width of the SMA window
     P = period of the cycle being averaged

The SMA is expressed in terms of wave amplitude. This mathematical equation for the frequency domain response of an SMA exactly describes the function shown in Figure 3.5, except that the figure is plotted in decibels rather than wave amplitude. Each time the ratio of the window width to the cycle period is an integer, the argument of the sine function is a multiple of Pi. Since the sine is exactly zero for arguments in multiples of Pi, the transfer response has nulls for these cycle periods.

Figure 3.5 shows that low-frequency components (longer cycles) are allowed to pass through the SMA with only a small amount of attenuation, or size reduction. However, high-frequency components (shorter cycles) are greatly attenuated, even between the null points. For this reason, an SMA falls into the category of low-pass filters. Low-pass filtering is exactly what is desired from a data smoother. The smoothing comes about as a result of reducing the size of, or *attenuating*, the amplitude of the higher-frequency components within the data.

The frequency description of an SMA does not have a null at zero frequency. At zero frequency, its period is infinite because cycle period is the reciprocal of frequency. Therefore, although the numerator goes to zero at zero frequency, the denominator also goes to zero. In the limit, the ratio of the numerator to the denominator is *unity* (a value of 1). We have previously assigned some significance to the cycle period that is twice the window width (or more precisely, where the window width was half the cycle period). In this case, the numerator in the SMA frequency description rises to become unity and the denominator is $\pi/2$. The cycle period that is twice the width of the SMA window is a workable and easy-to-remember demarcation between those cycle periods that have small attenuation and those that have greater attenuation. For example, an SMA window width of 8 bars would allow those cycle components of 16 bars and longer to pass nearly unattenuated and would attenuate cycle components whose periods are shorter than 16 bars.

We now have the tools to think about SMAs in both the time and frequency domains. We know that the 8-bar SMA has a lag of 3.5 bars for trends. This same SMA gives a 16-bar cycle a 90-degree phase delay and a 32-bar cycle a 45-degree phase delay. An 8-bar cycle component is removed completely. This ability to think of the impact of averages in both the time and frequency domains will greatly improve your probability of success as a trader.

Weighted Moving Average

A Weighted Moving Average (WMA) is closely related to an SMA. The major difference is the coefficients of the multiplier for the WMA are not constant across the window width. Rather, the coefficients are linearly weighted across the window. Therefore, it follows that the oldest data point is multiplied by 1, the next oldest data point is multiplied by 2, the third oldest data point is multiplied by 3, and so on until the most recent data point is multiplied by n for an n-bar window width. The sum of the data and coefficient products is divided by the sum of the coefficients to normalize the averaging process. A 4-bar WMA code can be written as

WMA = (4 * Price + 3 * Price[1] + 3 * Price[2] + Price[3])/10;

The transfer response of the 4-bar WMA is shown in Figure 3.6. Since the data are weighted across the window width, there can be no precise averaging to zero as there was with an SMA. Nevertheless, the WMA is also a low-pass filter. The point where the filter attenuation is 3 dB acts as our point of demarcation between the passband and the stopband. In Figure 3.6, this occurs at a normalized frequency of 0.25, corresponding to an 8-bar cycle. Cycles longer than roughly 8 bars are passed essentially unatten-

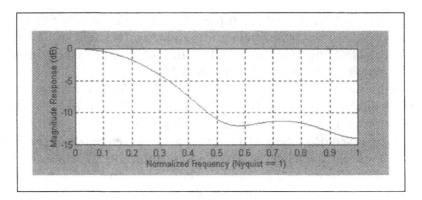

Figure 3.6.   Frequency response of a 4-bar WMA.

uated, and cycles shorter than 8 bars are reduced in amplitude to provide the smoothing.

As with SMAs, smoothing of WMAs is improved by increasing the width of the window. For example, the transfer response of a 7-bar WMA is shown in Figure 3.7. In this case, the −3 dB point occurs at a normalized frequency of about 0.14, which is a period of approximately 14 bars. Since the passband is linearly related to the window width, the passband of a WMA is also twice its window width, as a reasonable approximation.

A WMA offers a major advantage because it exhibits reduced lag in its transfer response. The reduced lag results from the

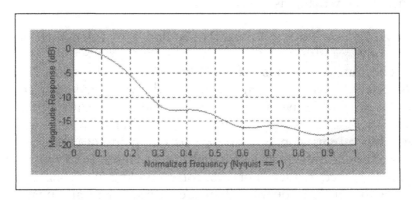

Figure 3.7.   Frequency response of a 7-bar WMA.

most recent data being the most heavily weighted. The amount of lag induced by an SMA or a WMA is the center of gravity of the transfer response. In the case of the SMA, the center of gravity is at the center of the filter, resulting in a lag of $(n - 1)/2$ for an n-bar window width. The shape of the WMA coefficients forms a triangle across the width of the filter, resulting in the center of gravity being a triangle, one-third of the distance across the window. Thus, the lag of an n-bar WMA is $(n - 1)/3$. Therefore, in our examples, a 4-bar WMA has a lag of only 1 bar and a 7-bar WMA has a lag of only 2 bars.

The weighting functions for a WMA do not necessarily have to be linear across the width of the window. The linear weighting is nonetheless very simple to compute, and the impact of linear weighting is easy to remember by recalling the center of gravity of a triangle. Furthermore, the impact of other weighting distributions is too subtle for trading purposes. Therefore, there is no compelling reason to use any weighting factor other than linear.

Exponential Moving Average

The moving averages discussed thus far are nonrecursive. That is, previous calculations are unnecessary to compute the current value of the moving average. An Exponential Moving Average (EMA) is different in a major way because it is recursive. The calculations use a fraction of the current price added to another fraction of the EMA calculation 1 bar ago. The first fraction is usually called alpha (α) and can have a value between 0 and 1. The two fractions must sum to unity, so the second fraction must have the value of $1 - \alpha$. The equation to compute an EMA is

$$EMA = \alpha * Price + (1 - \alpha) * EMA[1];$$

The EMA becomes a moving average by moving from bar to bar, from left to right, across the price data.

The term *exponential* describes the way an EMA transfer response decays in amplitude relative to a single input. Imagine a case in which the data set has an amplitude of $1/\alpha$ at one bar and an amplitude of 0 everywhere else. When the EMA is applied to this data, the first output from the filter is unity because there was no previous value for the EMA. On subsequent calculations, the price value is 0, and so the sequence of calculations is

$$EMA(0) = 1$$
$$EMA(1) = (1 - \alpha)$$
$$EMA(2) = (1 - \alpha)^{*}(1 - \alpha) = (1 - \alpha)^2$$
$$EMA(3) = (1 - \alpha)^{2*}(1 - \alpha) = (1 - \alpha)^3$$
$$\vdots$$
$$EMA(n) = (1 - \alpha)^n$$

Since the quantity $(1 - \alpha)$ must be less than 1, the amplitude decays as the exponent of each succeeding calculation from an impulse input. Hence the name Exponential. In principle, a part of any data input remains in subsequent calculations although the contribution becomes vanishingly small. This attribute makes an EMA part of a general class of filters called Infinite Impulse Response (IIR) filters. IIR filters are distinct from the Finite Impulse Response (FIR) filters, the class to which the SMA and WMA belong. With FIR filters, the filter provides an output only so long as the impulse falls within the window. Thus, in this case, the response to an impulse is finite.

It is instructive to examine the EMA response to a step function. A step function has a series of constant values and then jumps to another series of constant values. Assume the price has been 0 for a long time and then suddenly jumps up to a value of 1 and maintains that value thereafter. On the first bar, the EMA will have a value of α. On the second bar, the value will be $\alpha + \alpha^{*}(1 - \alpha)$. On the third bar, the value will be $\alpha + \alpha^{*}(1 - \alpha) + \alpha^{*}(1 - \alpha)^2$, and so on. The EMA will gradually approach the value of 1. A common error in programming is to insert a value for α, such as 0.2, and insert another number for $(1 - \alpha)$, such as 0.9. The two terms must sum to unity or the recursive algorithm will lead to erratic results or might even cause your computer to crash. You should always check your computer code to ensure the two terms sum to unity. I am so cautious on this point that I assign the value α as a global variable and write out the EMA equation in terms of α. By letting the computer do the work, I know the two terms must sum correctly.

We can easily derive the lag of an EMA for the case of price that rises linearly at the rate of one unit per bar. Recalling the form of the EMA calculation,

$$\text{EMA} = \alpha * \text{Price} + (1 - \alpha) * \text{EMA}[1];$$

We can assert that the price on day d is d. If we assume the lag of the EMA is L, then the current value of the EMA is $(d - L)$. Furthermore, the previous EMA would have a value of $(d - L - 1)$, since price is rising one unit per bar. Putting these values into the equation for the EMA, we obtain

$$
\begin{aligned}
(d - L) &= \alpha * d + (1 - \alpha) * (d - L - 1) \\
&= \alpha * d + (d - L) - 1 - \alpha * d + \alpha * (L + 1) \\
0 &= \alpha * (L + 1) - 1 \\
\alpha &= 1/(L + 1)
\end{aligned}
$$

This equation shows that we can select an acceptable lag, and from that lag, compute the alpha term of the EMA. For example, if we can accept a 3-bar lag resulting from the EMA, we would use α = 0.25.

We can also relate an EMA to an SMA on the basis of their equivalent static lags. Recalling that the lag of an SMA is $(n - 1)/2$ for an n-bar SMA, we can substitute this value of lag into the alpha calculation of the EMA as

$$
\begin{aligned}
\alpha &= 1/((n - 1)/2 + 1) \\
&= 2/((n - 1) + 2) \\
&= 2/(n + 1)
\end{aligned}
$$

This is the relationship between an n-bar SMA and the alpha of an EMA that is quoted in most technical analysis books.

A 12-bar SMA was used to compute the transfer response shown in Figure 3.5. The equivalent alpha for an EMA is α =

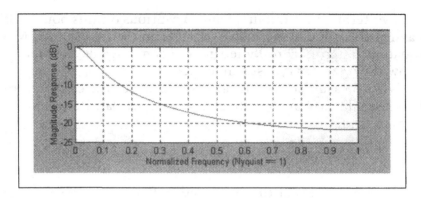

Figure 3.8. Transfer response of an EMA with delay equal to that of a 12-bar SMA.

$\frac{2}{13} = 0.1538$. The EMA transfer response for this value of alpha is shown in Figure 3.8. Comparing Figures 3.8 and 3.5, it is obvious that the EMA normalized frequency passband is much smaller than the passband of the SMA. Therefore, an EMA provides much more smoothing than an SMA for an equivalent amount of lag. Alternatively, you can conclude that an EMA has much less lag than an SMA for an equivalent amount of smoothing.

It is also interesting to compare a WMA to an EMA on the basis of equivalent lag. The WMA that produced the transfer response depicted in Figure 3.7 had a lag of 2 bars. For a 2-bar lag, an EMA has $\alpha = 0.3333$. The transfer response of the EMA is shown in Figure 3.9. In this case, the EMA response is nearly equivalent to the response of the WMA shown in Figure 3.7, with the WMA providing slightly better filtering. Furthermore, the WMA attenuates those components within the passband a little less than the EMA for these same components.

We do not yet have the tools to compute the cycle period of the passband demarcation in the frequency domain in terms of the alpha of the EMA, but we can assert without proof that this relationship is

$$P = -2\pi/\ln{(1 - \alpha)}$$

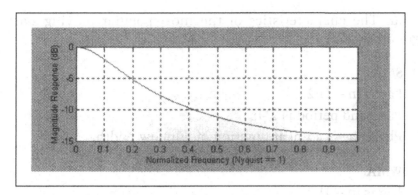

Figure 3.9. Transfer response of an EMA with delay equal to that of a 7-bar WMA.

where ln is the natural logarithm. This relationship is proved in Chapter 13. Computation of the natural logarithm may be unnatural to most traders, so we simplify the equation with a little mathematical slight of hand. We can approximate the natural logarithm with a truncated infinite series because $(1 - \alpha)$ will always be less than unity as

$$\ln (1 - \alpha) = -\alpha - \alpha^2/2 - \alpha^3/3 - \alpha^4/4 \ldots -\alpha^n/n$$

If α is sufficiently small, we can ignore all but the first two terms of the series. Substituting the truncated series for the natural logarithm in the passband period calculation, we obtain

$$P = 2\pi/(\alpha + \alpha^2/2)$$
$$= 4\pi/(\alpha^*(2 + \alpha))$$

Key Points to Remember

Regardless of their formulation, the purpose of moving averages is to smooth the input data. Their use is a trade-off between the amount of smoothing you desire and the amount of lag you can stand. The characteristics of the most popular moving averages are

SMA
Lag is $(n-1)/2$.
Passband period is $2*n$.
Phase lag is a linear function of window width.

WMA
Lag is $(n-1)/3$.
Passband period is $2*n$.
Gives the best filtering for a given amount of lag.
Phase lag is a linear function of window width.

EMA
$\alpha = 1/(Lag + 1)$.
$\alpha = 2/(n+1)$ when compared to an SMA.
The α and $(1 - \alpha)$ terms must always sum to unity.
Passband period is $-2\pi/\ln(1-\alpha) = 4\pi/(\alpha*(2+\alpha))$.
Phase lag is nonlinear due to recursion.

Chapter 4

MOMENTUM FUNCTIONS

Backward, turn backward,
oh time in your flight . . .

—Elizabeth Akers Allen

I can't begin to tell you the number of traders that has asked me to make their signals happen just one bar sooner. The typical question is "Can't you just take a momentum?" In the most simple case, momentum is just the 1-bar difference in price. Momentum is deceiving because it can give the illusion of anticipating turning points. In fact, there are cases in which some form of a momentum can increase the reaction time of an indicator. Even experienced technicians get lured into investigations in which advancing the indicator signal is impossible. For this reason, it is instructive to return to basics and thoroughly investigate the properties of momentum functions.

In the most general sense, momentum functions simply take the difference of successive values to sense the rate of change. Just as the sums forming the averages are analogous to integrals in the calculus, momentum is analogous to derivatives in the calculus. The impact of momentum can be appreciated by taking successive momentums as we do in Figure 4.1.

In Figure 4.1, we analyze the successive momentums of a simple ramp function. The ramp is described as having a zero slope before an instant in time T and then breaking to a finite slope at that instant. This is a relatively smooth function. The first momentum of the ramp is a step. There is no change in the slope of the ramp before or after time T, so the step function is

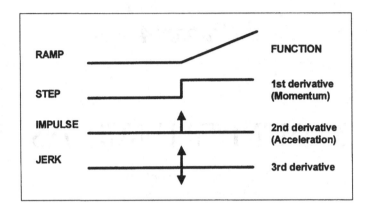

Figure 4.1.   Successive application of momentum shows that momentum can never anticipate an event. Also, momentum functions become increasingly discontinuous.

formed by instantly jumping from an initial slope of zero to the finite value of the slope of the ramp. Taking the momentum of the step function, there is no change except the instantaneous jump from one value to another at time *T*. This forms an impulse. An *impulse* is a mathematical artifice that has infinite height and zero width in such a way that the area of this "rectangle" is unity. Put simply, an impulse is a spike at time *T*. Next, taking the momentum of the impulse, we obtain a *jerk*. The jerk is formed by a two-step process. A positive impulse part of the jerk is first formed by traversing the leading edge of the impulse function. This is followed by the formation of the negative impulse part, which is due to traversing the trailing edge of the impulse function.

Examination of Figure 4.1 identifies two undeniable truths about momentum functions. These are

1. Momentum can never lead the event.
2. Momentum is always more disjoint (i.e., noisier) than the original function.

These truths are obvious when removed from the distractions of a price chart. There must be a reason why traders expect momentum to increase the performance of their indicators. That reason is demonstrated in Figure 4.2, where the momentum of a pure sine wave is taken. Since momentum is the rate of change of a function, the momentum of the sine wave is maximum at the left edge of Figure 4.2 where the sine wave crosses zero. The momentum decreases as the sine wave increases. It reaches zero at the point where the sine wave crests. The slope of the sine wave at this point is zero, causing the momentum to be zero. Continuing to the right, the slope of the sine wave increases in the negative direction, causing the momentum to reach its negative maximum just as the sine wave again crosses zero. The momentum is traced out by the dashed line in Figure 4.2. This dashed line has the characteristic that it reaches a crest 90 degrees before the sine wave crests and reaches a valley 90 degrees before the sine wave does.

If the price were a sine wave, it would be easy to conclude that momentum is a leading indicator. But this is true only when the market is in a Cycle Mode. It is, therefore, imperative to first identify the mode of the market before assigning a leading indicator capability to the momentum. In Chapter 11, methods to identify market modes are discussed.

We have already stated that momentum is analogous to a derivative in the calculus. We can use this fact to analyze the

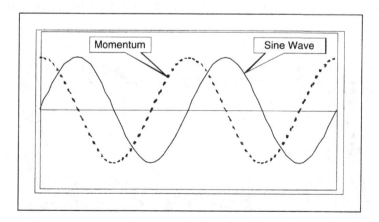

Figure 4.2.　Momentum leads a pure sine wave by 90 degrees.

behavior of momentum in the frequency domain. From any calculus text, the derivative of a sine wave having the angular frequency ω is

$$d(Sin(\omega t))/dt = \omega^* Cos(\omega t)$$

This equation shows that the derivative of a sine wave does lead the sine wave by 90 degrees because the result is exactly a cosine wave, like the dashed momentum shown in Figure 4.2. The equation also shows that amplitude is directly proportional to frequency. The amplitude is omega (ω), which is $2^*\pi^*$frequency. We expect the same phenomenon in trading. If we take the simple difference (momentum) of a 2-bar cycle that varies between +1 and −1, the difference will be the crest-to-valley value, or 2. Conversely, if we have a 50-bar cycle swinging between +1 and −1, then the maximum momentum will be approximately $^2/_{25} = 0.08$. There is no momentum for extremely long cycles because there is essentially no rate of change that is useful for trading. The frequency response of a simple 1-bar momentum is shown in Figure 4.3.

Figure 4.3 shows that a zero frequency signal is almost completely rejected by the filter. Shorter frequencies are rejected less. For example, a 10-bar cycle signal has a normalized frequency of 2/Period = $^2/_{10} = 0.2$, and is only attenuated by about 10 dB. A 4-bar cycle signal ($^2/_4 = 0.5$ normalized frequency) is only

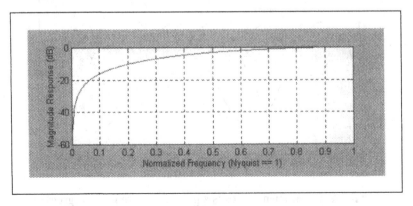

Figure 4.3. Frequency response of a simple momentum.

attenuated by about 3 dB. Since very-low-frequency components are rejected and higher-frequency components are passed, Figure 4.3 suggests that momentum can be used as a detrending filter. However, the passband is too narrow to be of practical benefit. As you recall from Chapter 3, the half-power point, or –3 dB point, is the accepted practical cutoff frequency. According to this definition, only cycles with periods of 4 bars or less would be pass. We can flatten the frequency response by making the filter wider. However, in making the filter wider we also increase the lag. As with an SMA, the lag through an n-bar momentum is Lag = $(n - 1)/2$. Therefore, there is a 1-bar lag for a 3-bar momentum (Lag = $(3 - 1)/2 = 2/2 = 1$). The 3-bar momentum is computed from the equation:

$$Mo = 0.5 * Price - 0.5 * Price[2];$$

The frequency response of this filter is shown in Figure 4.4. There are two clear benefits from this filter, as opposed to the simple momentum filter of Figure 4.3. First, the frequency response of the filter is much flatter. For example, the attenuation at the normalized frequency of 0.1 (a 20-bar cycle) is only –10 dB instead of the approximate –17 dB in Figure 4.3. Second, the 2-bar cycle (normalized frequency = 1) is nearly completely suppressed. The 2-bar cycle is always suppressed if the order of the symmetrical filter is odd.

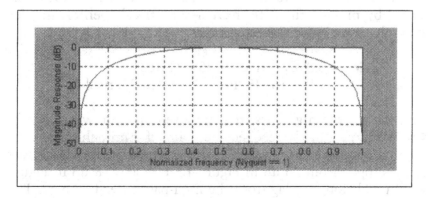

Figure 4.4. A 3-bar detrending filter has flatter frequency response and rejects the 2-bar cycle.

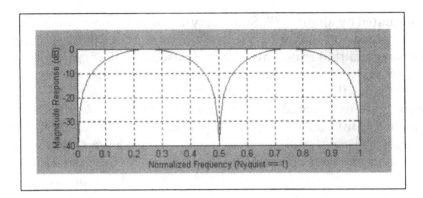

Figure 4.5. A 5-bar momentum removes both 2- and 4-bar cycle components.

If a little bit is good, a whole lot more is better—maybe. We can attempt to flatten the frequency response by using a 5-bar momentum. The equation becomes

$$Mo = 0.5 * Price - 0.5 * Price[4];$$

The frequency response for this 5-bar momentum is shown in Figure 4.5. Unfortunately, we have introduced another frequency notch at a 4-bar cycle. Once we stop and think about it, we see that this makes sense because subtracting data from a 4-bar cycle 4 bars ago will exactly cancel any output from the high-pass filter.

The frequency notching exhibited in Figure 4.5 can be eliminated by making the filter have symmetrical coefficients. For example, if we write the equation as

$$Mo = 0.0909 * Price + 0.4545 * Price[1]$$
$$+ 0 - 0.4545 * Price[3] - 0.0909 * Price[4];$$

we then get the high-pass frequency response shown in Figure 4.6. We have quickly reached the point of diminishing returns for this approach. For example, the attenuation for the 20-bar cycle slipped from –5 dB in Figure 4.5 to about –8 dB in Figure 4.6. In addition, the lag from the high-pass filter is 3 bars. The

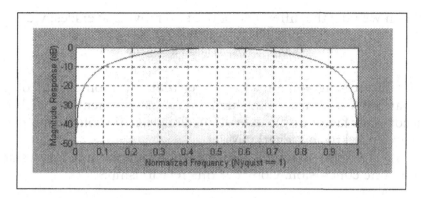

Figure 4.6. A 5-bar high-pass filter smoothes passband frequency response.

advantage of the 90-degree phase lead due to differencing is quickly lost due to the lag. The total phase lag as a function of cycle period due to the 3-bar lag can be written as

$$\text{Phase lag} = 360*3/\text{Period} -90 \text{ degrees}$$

By setting the phase lag to zero, we find that the shortest cycle period having no phase lag is a 12-bar period. Longer cycles will have a phase lead. Since we need to work with cycle periods even shorter than 12 bars, there is no point in attempting to make the differencing have a wider passband because additional lag will be induced. Thus, we have reached our point of diminishing returns. Further amplitude corrections must be accomplished by measuring the dominant cycle and then applying a correction term for that cycle.

It is interesting to take the momentum of an SMA. To clarify this point, we refer to prices from the current time as A, B, C, D, and E. A 4-bar SMA of the prices is

$$\text{SMA} = (A + B + C + D)/4$$

and the 4-bar SMA of the prices 1 bar ago is

$$\text{SMA}[1] = (B + C + D + E)/4$$

When we take the difference of the two moving averages, we get

$$SMA - SMA[1] = (A - E)/4$$

The interesting conclusion here is that the momentum of a 4-bar SMA is exactly the same as a 4-bar momentum within a constant factor of the averaging. This specific conclusion can be extended to any length SMA.

By the same token, an SMA of four momentums arrives at the same conclusion. Consider this relationship:

$$((A - B) + (B - C) + (C - D) + (D - E))/4 = (A - E)/4$$

It all boils down to the same thing. An *n*-bar average of momentums is exactly the same as an *n*-bar momentum.

Key Points to Remember

- Momentum can never lead the event.
- Momentum is always noisier than the original function.
- Momentum can produce a 90-degree phase lead in the Cycle Mode.
- Improving momentum quickly reaches a point of diminishing returns.
- Amplitude compensation of momentum can be accomplished by measuring the dominant cycle and applying a correction for that cycle period.
- The momentum of an *n*-bar SMA is the same as an *n*-bar momentum.

Chapter 5

COMPLEX VARIABLES

Numbers are like people; torture them enough
and they will tell you anything.

—Anonymous

The mathematical concept of complex variables is introduced in this chapter to lay the groundwork for the derivation of indicators that are either impossible without complex variables or that would require enormous computational overhead without them. Mastering complex variables will give you great insight into the way market action can be described, and can even suggest new indicators.

Since you are reading this book, you are undoubtedly comfortable with our number system. However, there are some primitive societies that have no words for numbers larger than 10, other than an equivalent to "many," because they run out of fingers on which to count. Even more surprising is the fact that the concept of zero is a relatively modern invention. If you stop and think about it, "nothing" in the physical world is an abstract concept, so why would one need a word to describe it? There was no zero in Roman numerals. In fact, the concept of zero was not introduced to the Western world until the Renaissance when Leonardo de Pisa (1170–1240) (also called Fibonacci) wrote *Liber abaci.* Somewhat later, the idea of negative numbers was introduced. If zero is an abstract concept, how could one possibly have less than nothing? Clearly, this objection to the number system existed before the days of margin calls. Today, it is accepted that the numbering system can be viewed as a continuum of real numbers ranging from minus infinity to plus infinity along a straight line.

There is no reason why numbers must be confined to a line. We can conceive of numbers as existing in a plane. Following this concept, any position on that plane can be described by an ordered pair of real numbers. The first number of the pair denotes the number of units along the horizontal dimension, and the second number of the pair denotes the number of units along the vertical dimension. But describing a position in a plane is rather clumsy. Also, a need for complex numbers arises in algebra from the impossibility of finding the square roots of negative quantities. The clumsy situation has to be avoided, and we do this by the invention of the imaginary unit

$$i = \sqrt{-1}$$

We can then define a *complex number* as a combination of $(a + ib)$ formed from the two real numbers a and b, and the imaginary unit i. The imaginary unit i not only has the value of the square root of -1, but also serves as a rotation operator. Thus, the point on the plane denoted by $(a + ib)$ is a units along the horizontal and b units along the vertical. In this structure, the imaginary operator reorients a real number from the horizontal axis to the vertical, acting as the rotation operator. The two components a and ib are called the real and the imaginary, respectively, of the complex number. Numbers along the vertical dimension are often called imaginary numbers. This is an unfortunate name choice, for this number is no more imaginary than other numbers. Imaginary numbers is just an assigned name, like rational numbers or prime numbers. What is important is that the use of complex numbers ensures that a polynomial of any order with real coefficients can be factored into complex roots. For example, the polynomial $x^2 + bx + c$ cannot be factored into real roots if $c > b^2$.

Electrical engineering uses the symbol i to denote electrical current. Therefore, it is common practice to use the symbol j to denote the complex operator to avoid confusion with electrical current. We follow that practice in this book. It is also common to refer to the horizontal dimension as x and the vertical dimen-

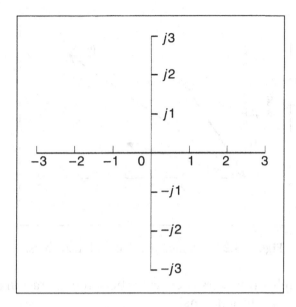

Figure 5.1. Real and imaginary numbers in the complex plane.

sion as y, so the complex number z is understood to be $z = x + jy$. The real and complex numbers forming the complex plane are depicted in Figure 5.1.

Arithmetic can be easily performed in the complex plane. If you add a real number to another real number, the result is a real number that is the sum of the two real numbers. If you add an imaginary number to another imaginary number, the result is an imaginary number that is the sum of the two imaginary numbers. However, if you add an imaginary number to a real number, the result is a complex number. The real numbers and imaginary numbers are said to be *orthogonal*. In this case, orthogonal not only means that the numbers exist at right angles, but it also means that they are independent of each other. The most complicated mathematical operation occurs when a complex number is added to another complex number. In doing this, the real components are added together and, independently, the imaginary components are added together. An example of complex addition is shown in Figure 5.2, which shows that the addi-

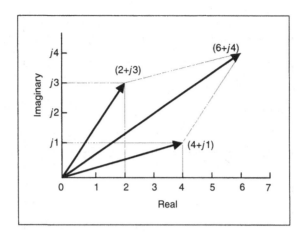

Figure 5.2.   Addition of two complex numbers.

tion of complex numbers is exactly the same operation as vector addition in two dimensions.

The product of a real and an imaginary number is imaginary. Thus $2*j3 = j6$. The product of two real numbers is real, as is the product of two imaginary numbers: $j2*j3 = -6$, and $j3*(-j4) = +12$. The reason the product of two imaginary numbers is real is that the imaginary unit is also multiplied, and $j^2 = -1$. The multiplication of two generalized complex numbers is

$$(a + jb)*(c + jd) = ac - bd + jad + jbc = (ac - bd) + j(ad + bc)$$

A complex number can also be expressed in polar coordinates. With reference to Figure 5.3, the polar coordinate dimensions are r at an angle of θ. The relationships between the real and imaginary coordinates and the polar coordinates are

$$a = r*\text{Cos}(\theta)$$
$$b = r*\text{Sin}(\theta)$$
$$r = \sqrt{a^2 + b^2}$$
$$\theta = \text{ArcTan}(b/a)$$

It is also useful to express complex numbers in exponential form. The exponential function is, by definition, equal to the limit approached by an infinite series:

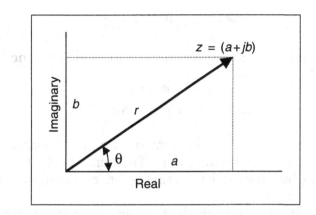

Figure 5.3. Components of z.

$$e^x = 1 + x + \frac{x^2}{2!} + \frac{x^3}{3!} + \ldots \frac{x^n}{n!}$$

This series reminds us of the series that defines the trigonometric functions:

$$\cos(\theta) = 1 - \frac{\theta^2}{2!} + \frac{\theta^4}{4!} - \ldots + (-1)^n \frac{\theta^{2n}}{(2n)!}$$

$$\sin(\theta) = \theta - \frac{\theta^3}{3!} + \frac{\theta^5}{5!} - \ldots - (-1)^{2n-1} \frac{\theta^{(2n-1)}}{(2n-1)!}$$

The sine and cosine series, although rather like the exponential series in most other ways, have a reversal of sign of alternate terms. A similar reversal of sign takes place in the exponential series, but only if the exponent is imaginary. Consider $e^{j\theta}$, which can be found by letting $x = j\theta$ in the exponential series. In this case we obtain

$$e^{j\theta} = \left(1 - \frac{\theta^2}{2!} + \frac{\theta^4}{4!} - \ldots\right) + j\left(\theta - \frac{\theta^3}{3!} + \frac{\theta^5}{5!} - \ldots\right)$$

By comparison to the series expansions for the sine and cosine functions, we can express the exponential form as

$$e^{j\theta} = \text{Cos}\ (\theta) + j\ \text{Sin}\ (\theta)$$

Alternately, we can express the Cosine and Sine functions as

$$e^{j\theta} + e^{-j\theta} = 2\ \text{Cos}\ (\theta)$$
$$\text{and}\quad e^{j\theta} - e^{-j\theta} = j2\ \text{Sin}\ (\theta)$$

This is an important theorem of complex variable theory known as *Euler's Theorem*. Euler's Theorem says that sines and cosines can be expressed in terms of an exponential function having an imaginary operator.

We are all familiar with the frequency of a cycle. For example, the power coming from our wall plugs is an alternating current. The frequency of this alternating current is 60 cycles per second. Cycles are repetitive. Each time a cycle is completed, it sweeps through 360 degrees, or 2π radians, of a sine wave. It is convenient to define the *angular frequency* as 2π times the regular frequency by the equation $\omega = 2\pi f$, where ω is the Greek letter omega. Using these definitions, ωt is the number of radians a cycle covers in a given amount of time. Since ωt is an angle, we can represent the cycle in exponential form as $e^{j\omega t}$, using complex notation. We thus see in Figure 5.4 that a pure cycle of an analytic waveform in the time domain can be represented as a projection onto either the real or imaginary axis.

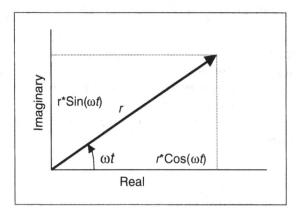

Figure 5.4. Exponential complex frequency and its components.

The concept of the exponential form is an extremely important one for the digital signal processing of trading waveforms. The waveform we observe on the charts is called an *analytic waveform*. If we can break the analytic waveform into its two orthogonal components, we can immediately find the amplitude of the cycle. By examination of Figure 5.4 and using the Pythagorean Theorem, we can see that the square of the real component plus the square of the imaginary component is equal to r^2, the square of the cycle amplitude. Thus, we have a bar-by-bar measurement of the amplitude of the cycle in the time domain. Such a highly responsive measurement of signal amplitude is an important component of all effective trading indicators and systems.

The exponential form also gives us a particularly simple way to measure the period of the market cycle. The cycle period measurement approach can be understood with reference to Figure 5.5. The initial measurement is made at time t_1 so that the phase angle is ωt_1. The second measurement is made at time t_2, resulting in the measured angle ωt_2. The difference between the two phase angles is $\Delta\theta$. To measure the cycle period, we simply keep adding all the $\Delta\theta$s until the sum equals 360 degrees. The number of times we have to add the $\Delta\theta$s is, by definition, the period of the cycle. We discuss exactly how to do this in Chapter 7.

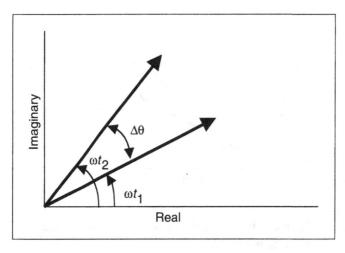

Figure 5.5. Two successive phasor measurements.

Figures 5.4 and 5.5 are phasor diagrams. Phasor diagrams represent the cycle as a rotating vector (or, the phasor) in complex coordinates, where the tail of the phasor is pinned to the origin. The length of the phasor represents the wave amplitude of the cycle. The phase angle represents a particular location within the cycle.

The phasor diagrams we have been discussing only consider the presence of one significant dominant cycle in the data. Happily, that is usually the case. The phasor diagram is therefore useful for comparing the lead and amplitude of momentum functions to the original data, and also for comparing the lag and amplitude of smoothing functions to the original data.

But what if there is a secondary cycle present in the data? Such a cycle is very difficult to identify because it lasts for only a brief amount of time and the short amount of data we are forced to use cannot provide enough resolution for filters. Since the complex variables can be added, the phasor picture might look something like the depiction in Figure 5.6. The dominant cycle, having a frequency of ω_1, is rotating as previously described. The secondary cycle is assumed to have a smaller amplitude and a higher frequency ω_2. When these two complex variables are added, the secondary cycle spins like a bicycle pedal at the end of the crank, which is analogous to the tip of the phasor of the first

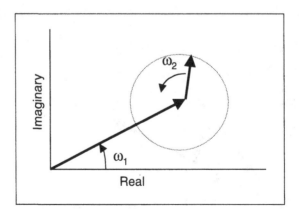

Figure 5.6 The addition of two phasors having different frequencies.

cycle. Assuming the secondary cycle is present only for a short while, the resultant phasor will look like the dominant cycle with a little whiffle superimposed on it. These whiffles are immediately identifiable when the phasor is plotted. In later chapters, we identify these whiffles in the real data.

Key Points to Remember

- Complex variables are a two-dimensional number set.
- The horizontal dimensions are called real numbers.
- The vertical dimensions are called imaginary numbers.
- $j = \sqrt{-1}$ and is the 90-degree rotation operator.
- A rotating phasor describes a pure cycle from the exponential complex frequency.
- Relative phases can be described using phasor diagrams.
- Euler's equations describe Cosines and Sines of real frequencies as being comprised of complex frequencies.
- Two simultaneous cycles can be depicted as a bicycle diagram.

Chapter 6

HILBERT TRANSFORMS

Ideas are like rabbits. You get a couple
and learn how to handle them,
and pretty soon you have a dozen.

—John Steinbeck

This chapter contains some of the most important concepts upon which all the following practical applications are based. First, we derive the Hilbert Transform. The *Hilbert Transform* is a procedure to create complex signals from the simple chart data familiar to all traders. Once we have the complex signals, we can compute indicators and signals that are more accurate and responsive than those computed using conventional techniques. In fact, some of the indicators we will discuss cannot be calculated at all without the Hilbert Transform.

If we accept that there can be imaginary numbers, then the concept of negative frequencies should pose no problem. If we review trigonometric identities, we recall that $\text{Cos}(-\omega t) = \text{Cos}(\omega t)$ and that $\text{Sin}(-\omega t) = -\text{Sin}(\omega t)$. These identities show that we can easily accommodate negative frequencies. Further, the power contained in waveforms is proportional to the average square of the waveform. The squaring of the sign always produces a positive power, so there can be no exception to the concept of conservation of power if we use negative frequencies.

When data are sampled at a sampling frequency f_s, that sampling frequency acts like a radio carrier signal. That is, the real data being sampled are heterodyned into upper and lower sidebands of the sampling frequency. Mathematically, heterodyning is multiplying two frequencies (and then filtering to select the desired output). So, if we have a baseband data frequency of f_b, the heterodyning can be described as the product of two signals. By a trigonometric identity, this product results in the sum and difference frequencies as

$$0.5*Cos(2\pi f_s t)*Cos(2\pi f_b t) = Cos(2\pi(f_s + f_b)t) + Cos(2\pi(f_s - f_b)t)$$

The lower sideband can be considered as a negative frequency relative to the sampling frequency, and the upper sideband can be considered as a positive frequency relative to the sampling frequency. Furthermore, every harmonic of the sampling frequency exists. Each harmonic also has an upper and lower sideband containing the baseband signals.

Since the lower sideband of the sampling frequency exists, it could extend down into the baseband range of frequencies. For this reason, the baseband range of frequencies is limited to $f_s/2$. This is called the *Nyquist sampling criteria*. In trading, this means the absolute shortest period we can use is a 2-bar cycle, or a frequency of 0.5 cycles per bar. The sampling frequency can be weekly, daily, hourly, and so on, but the shortest period we can consider in any time frame is a 2-bar cycle.

The sampled data spectrum can be pictured as shown in Figure 6.1. The baseband signal is depicted as a continuum of frequencies that is bandlimited, either naturally or by a filter, to be less than half the sampling frequency f_s. Several of the harmonics of the sampling frequency are also shown, along with their respective sidebands. Since we are talking about complex functions, the sampled spectrum can extend below zero frequency as well. As a result, the complete sampled frequency spectrum extends from minus infinity to plus infinity, as shown in Figure 6.2. An interesting observation is that either the upper or lower sideband of any harmonic of the sampling frequency can be processed with exactly the same result because the same information resides in all sidebands. The frequency selection for processing is a matter of convenience and is, therefore, usually the baseband because demodulation of the zero frequency harmonic is not required.

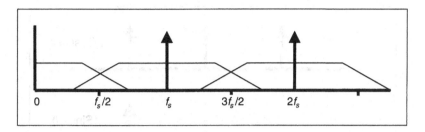

Figure 6.1. The baseband frequency below half the sampling frequency appears as sidebands on harmonics of the sampling frequency.

The waveforms with which all traders are familiar are called *analytic signals.* Analytic signals are defined as a special case of a complex function without imaginary values, that have only positive or only negative frequencies, but not both. We need to construct more general complex functions to enable more efficient signal processing. This can be done by synthesizing the analytic signal from a combination of two complex signals that are odd and even functions around zero.

First, we must recall the trigonometric identities $\text{Cos}(\omega t) = \text{Cos}(-\omega t)$ and $\text{Sin}(\omega t) = -\text{Sin}(-\omega t)$ and Euler's equations:

$$e^{j\omega t} + e^{-j\omega t} = 2\,\text{Cos}(\omega t)$$

and
$$e^{j\omega t} - e^{-j\omega t} = j2\,\text{Sin}(\omega t)$$

We can synthesize the analytic signal by summing the two complex signals as shown in Figure 6.3. The real component of Figure 6.3(a) is summed with the imaginary component in Figure 6.3(b) to form the complex signal shown in Figure 6.3(c). From Euler's

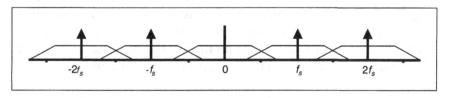

Figure 6.2. Sampled data spectrum extends to negative frequencies.

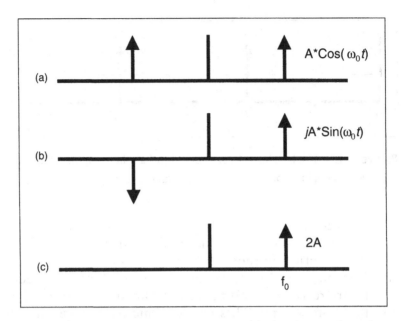

Figure 6.3. An analytic signal is comprised of InPhase and Quadrature components.

equations, the two complex signals can be called the InPhase (i.e., the Cosine) component and the Quadrature (i.e., the Sine) component. *Quadrature* means being rotated by 90 degrees.

The Hilbert Transformer has been derived in a number of texts, to which you may want to refer for more information.[1] One purpose of a Hilbert Transform is to create a complex signal from an analytic signal. A Hilbert Transformer shifts all positive frequencies by −90 degrees and all negative frequencies by 90 degrees. Since the frequency response of sampled systems is periodic, we can describe the Hilbert Transformer in terms of angular frequency as shown in Figure 6.4 for unity amplitude components. Since this graph is periodic, we can use the Fourier series to determine the coefficients of the exponential series that represents the plot. The Fourier series can be written as

---

[1]Rabiner, Lawrence R., and Bernard Gold. *Theory and Application of Digital Signal Processing.* Englewood Cliffs: Prentice Hall, 1975.

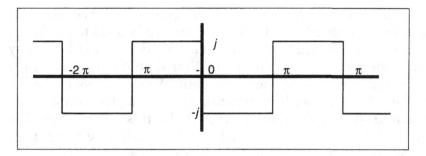

Figure 6.4. Periodic frequency response of a Digital Hilbert Transformer.

$$H(z) = \sum_{n=-\infty}^{\infty} C_n Z^n$$

If we let $z = e^{j\omega T}$ with $T = 1$, the Fourier Transform becomes

$$C_n = \frac{1}{2\pi} \int_{-\pi}^{\pi} H(e^{j\omega}) e^{-jn\omega} d\omega$$

and

$$H(e^{j\omega}) = \sum_{n=-\infty}^{\infty} C_n e^{j\omega n}$$

This equation describes the coefficients of the digital filter. Solving the integral equation for the filter coefficients (because the square wave has the same $\mathrm{Sin}(x)/x$ form as the pulse described in Chapter 3), we obtain

$$C_n = \frac{2}{\pi} \frac{\mathrm{Sin}^2\left(\frac{\pi n}{2}\right)}{n}$$

for $n \neq 0$ and $C_n = 0$ for $n = 0$.

The value of n is relative to the center of the filter, so the center coefficient is always zero. The value of the sine squared term is always positive and has a unity value for odd values of n. The coefficients are, therefore, simply $1/n$ for odd values of n; they are positive for the most recent data half of the filter; and they are negative in the older data half of the filter. The ideal Hilbert Transformer extends coefficients from minus infinity to plus infinity. The $2/\pi$ factor can be ignored here because each coefficient is divided by the sum of the coefficients to produce a normalized amplitude response. That is, the desired frequency components at the output of the filter should have the sample amplitude they had at the filter input. We can approximate the Hilbert Transformer by truncating the extent. For example, we could truncate the filter at $n = 7$. In this case, where the detrended Price is represented by P, the Quadrature component (Q) of the Hilbert Transform can be written as

$$Q = (P/7 + P[2]/5 + P[4]/3 + P[6] - P[8] - P[10]/3 - P[12]/5 - P[14]/7)/(1 + 1/3 + 1/5 + 1/7);$$

The InPhase component (I) of the filter is referenced to the center of the filter, and can be written simply as

$$I = P[7]$$

Note that the lag of this Hilbert Transform is 7 bars.

Since the Hilbert Transformer must be truncated, ideally it should be sufficiently long to capture a full cycle of the longest period under consideration. It is not unreasonable to want to process a cycle that is 40-bars long. This is about two months of daily data. In this case, we would like to truncate at $n = 19$. However, such a Hilbert Transformer would have a lag of 21 bars. This lag is unacceptable because we would also want to process cycles with a period of 10 bars or less. The 21-bar lag would be more than two cycles of the data that have shorter periods.

An alternative way to truncate the Hilbert Transformer is to use as short a filter as possible. If we truncate the Hilbert Transformer at $n = 3$, the Quadrature component can be written as

$$Q = (P/3 + P[2] - P[4] - P[6]/3)/(4/3)$$
$$= 0.25*P + 0.75*P[2] - 0.75*P[4] - 0.25*P[6];$$

This short Hilbert Transformer has a lag of only 3 bars. However, the severe truncation produces the amplitude transfer response shown in Figure 6.5. A truncated Hilbert Transformer has a frequency response similar to that of a momentum function.

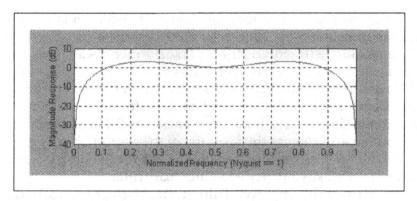

Figure 6.5. Amplitude response of a Hilbert Transformer truncated at $n = 3$.

The amplitude response of a minimum-length Hilbert Transformer can be improved by adjusting the filter coefficients by trial and error. The resulting Hilbert Transformer filter equation is

$$Q = 0.0962*P + 0.5769*P[2] - 0.5769*P[4] - 0.0962*P[6];$$

The amplitude response of the Improved Hilbert Transformer is shown in Figure 6.6.

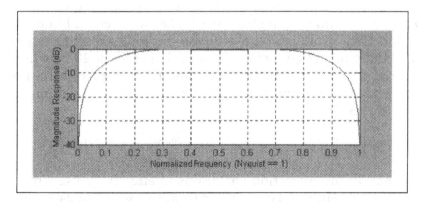

Figure 6.6. Amplitude response of the Improved Hilbert Transformer.

The response of the Improved Hilbert Transformer is not dissimilar from the 5-bar high-pass filter described in Chapter 4 (Figure 4.6). The Improved Hilbert Transformer has a more symmetrical response, but has a 3-bar lag versus the 2-bar lag of the high-pass filter. Also, there is less rejection of the intermediate-length cycles in the Improved Hilbert Transformer. For example, the attenuation for a normalized frequency of 0.1 (a 20-bar cycle) is about −6 dB, whereas the rejection of the 5-bar high-pass filter was about −8 dB at this frequency. The Improved Hilbert Transformer also makes a pretty good high-pass filter.

We formed the Improved Hilbert Transformer to satisfy the criterion of minimizing lag. The penalty we paid for minimizing lag was the resulting amplitude taper across the frequency band at which we desire to operate. Since the Improved Hilbert Transformer is so similar to a high-pass filter, and the high-pass filter has an amplitude rolloff directly proportional to frequency, we can compensate for the amplitude rolloff if we know the frequency. We do not have the frequency directly because we need the InPhase and Quadrature components to compute it. However, we do know what the measured cycle period was 1 bar ago. Since frequency is a slowly varying function from bar to bar, the cycle period 1 bar ago can easily be used for amplitude compensation.

If the Hilbert Transformer were a pure differentiator, we know the amplitude correction term would be inversely proportional to ω (see Chapter 4). Since the cycle period is the reciprocal of the frequency, the correction term would be (Period/2π). When we examine Figure 6.6, we see that we need an 11 dB correction for a cycle period of 40 bars (normalized frequency of 0.05) and a 6.2 dB correction for a cycle period of 20 bars (normalized frequency of 0.1). Converting these decibel values to amplitude and writing a straight line correction equation, we have the result

Amplitude correction = (0.075 * Period[1] + 0.54)

This amplitude correction enables us to effectively use a minimum-length Hilbert Transformer to keep the lag to as small a value as possible.

The purpose of the Hilbert Transform, as explained earlier, is to create InPhase and Quadrature components from the analytic waveform. The InPhase and Quadrature components enable efficient computation to find the dominant cycle period, the dominant cycle amplitude, and the phase of the dominant cycle. From these parameters we can calculate unique and precise indicators, such as the *Signal-to-Noise Ratio*, the Sinewave Indicator (a Cycle Mode predictive indicator), and an Instantaneous Trendline. The (nearly) complete code to calculate the InPhase and Quadrature components is given in Figure 6.7. (The complete code requires the computation of the dominant cycle period, which is covered in the next chapter.)

In EasyLanguage code, all input values must be defined. In the case of Figure 6.7, the only input value is Price, and is computed as the average of the High and Low for each bar in the data

```
Inputs:      Price((H+L)/2);

Vars:  Smooth(0), Detrender(0), I1(0), Q1(0), Period(0);

If CurrentBar > 5 then begin
     Smooth = (4*Price + 3*Price[1] + 2*Price[2] +
        Price[3]) / 10;
     Detrender = (.0962*Smooth + .5769*Smooth[2] -
        .5769*Smooth[4] - .0962*Smooth[6])*
        (.075*Period[1] + .54);

     {Compute InPhase and Quadrature components}
     Q1 = (.0962*Detrender + .5769*Detrender[2] -
        .5769*Detrender[4] - .0962*Detrender[6])*
        (.075*Period[1] + .54);
     I1 = Detrender[3];

     Plot1(I1, "InPhase");
     Plot2(-Q1, "Quadrature);

End;
```

Figure 6.7. Hilbert Transform EasyLanguage code.

series. Next, all the other variables must be defined, and their initial values must be set to zero. The first line of computational code computes the variable Smoother as a 4-bar Weighted Moving Average (WMA) of Price. A 4-bar WMA is used to remove some of the higher-frequency components prior to detrending the Price. The lag penalty for this smoothing is only 1 bar. The Price is detrended in the next line of code. Since we have an amplitude-corrected Hilbert Transformer, and since we want to detrend over its length, we simply use the Hilbert Transformer itself as the detrender. We do not particularly care about the phase of the detrended analytic signal at this point. However, we do note that detrending has introduced another 3 bars of lag into the computation. The amplitude correction can be applied after we compute the period of the dominant cycle. The InPhase and Quadrature components are contained in the next two lines of code. The Quadrature component is computed by applying the Hilbert Transformer a second time. The InPhase component is computed simply by using the Detrender value referenced to 3 bars ago, the center of the Hilbert Transformer. Therefore, the calculation of the InPhase and Quadrature components introduces still another 3 bars of delay in the calculation. We now have a total of 7 bars of delay after computing the InPhase and Quadrature components.

The InPhase and Quadrature components are only concerned with Cycle Mode signals because the Detrender removed the trending components. The 7-bar lag can be converted to a phase lag by the following process: We divide the 7-bar lag by the dominant cycle period to get a percentage of a cycle and then multiply by 360 degrees. Furthermore, the Hilbert Transformer offers the advantage of providing 90 degrees of phase lead. The equation for phase lag is then

$$\text{Phase lag} = 360 * 7 / \text{Period} - 90$$

Therefore, a 28-bar dominant cycle will have zero lag. A 14-bar dominant cycle will have 90 degrees lag, or a quarter cycle. The phase lag grows rapidly for still shorter cycle periods. For example, a 7-bar cycle will have 180-degrees lag, corresponding to a half cycle. The phase lag of the InPhase and Quadrature components can be a serious consideration when interpreting the results of some indicators. For example, knowing the InPhase component is delayed by 7 bars from the time-domain waveform, we can anticipate the crest of the time-domain waveform by projecting when the InPhase component will reach its maximum 7 bars into the future.

Key Points to Remember

- Both positive and negative frequencies are possible in signal processing.
- Only positive frequencies or only negative frequencies, but not both, comprise the analytic signal.
- Complex signals contain InPhase and Quadrature components.
- An analytic signal can be synthesized by complex signals.
- Following the preceding two points, an analytic signal can be decomposed into InPhase and Quadrature components.
- A Hilbert Transformer is the technique used to decompose analytic signals.
- Hilbert Transformers must be severely truncated to produce acceptable lag for use in trading.
- Amplitude compensation of the InPhase and Quadrature components can be accomplished by knowing the period of the dominant cycle.
- The analytic signal must be smoothed and detrended prior to computing the InPhase and Quadrature components.
- The amplitude-compensated Hilbert Transformer can be used to detrend the analytic waveform.
- The phase lag of the InPhase and Quadrature components is (360*7/Period – 90) degrees.

Chapter 7

MEASURING CYCLE PERIODS

*. . . but what are we going to do with
all those skinned cats?*

—A<small>NONYMOUS</small>

One fundamental definition of a cycle is that the process under consideration has a constant rate of phase change. We can measure the phase of a complex signal directly. Knowing the phase at each sample, we need only take the bar-to-bar difference to obtain the rate of phase change. In this chapter, you are presented with several mathematical techniques for measuring the period of the dominant cycle. While mathematically dissimilar, all these techniques share the common feature of using differential phase between samples.

Phase Accumulation

The Phase Accumulation technique of cycle period measurement is perhaps the easiest to comprehend. In this technique, we measure the phase at each sample by taking the arctangent of the ratio of the Quadrature component to the InPhase component. A delta phase is generated by taking the difference of the phase between successive samples. At each sample we can then look backward, adding up the delta phases. When the sum of the delta phases reaches 360 degrees, we must have passed through one full cycle, on average. The process is repeated for each new sample.

The Phase Accumulation method of cycle measurement always uses one full cycle's worth of historical data. This is both an advantage and disadvantage. The advantage is the lag in obtaining the answer scales directly with the cycle period. That is, the measurement of a short cycle period has less lag than the measurement of a longer cycle period. However, the number of samples used in making the measurement means the averaging period is variable with cycle period. Longer averaging reduces the noise level compared to the signal. Therefore, shorter cycle periods necessarily have a higher output Signal-to-Noise Ratio.

Implementing the Phase Accumulation method of cycle measurement with the EasyLanguage code is described with reference to Figure 7.1. The initial part of the code creates the InPhase and Quadrature components, I1 and Q1, as discussed in the last chapter. It is crucial that I1 and Q1 be smoothed before the arctangent of their ratio is taken. We do the smoothing in an EMA whose alpha equals 0.15. The *instantaneous phase* (the phase at any bar) is computed as the arctangent of the ratio of Q1 to I1. This gives the instantaneous phase within a quadrant. The quadrant ambiguity is removed in the subsequent three lines of code. We then compute the differential phase (DeltaPhase) between successive samples. There can be considerable error in the raw differential phase computation. To keep these large errors from unduly influencing the outcome, we limit the values of the differential phase to be between cycle periods of 6 bars (DeltaPhase = $\frac{360}{6}$ = 60) and 50 bars (Delta Phase = $\frac{360}{50}$ = 7). The DeltaPhases are then accumulated until the PhaseSum exceeds 360 degrees. At that point, the cycle period is assigned as the number of samples required for the PhaseSum to reach the 360-degree value. The accumulation is done for each bar in the data set but is limited to a value of 40 bars. The limitation is based on our assumption that cycle periods of 40 bars and longer result in a Trend Mode, and detailed knowledge of their periods is not necessary. If the cycle period has not been identified within the maximum 40-bar accumulation period, then it is assigned the value of the cycle period measurement for the previous sample. It is then smoothed by an EMA whose alpha equals 0.25 to create a pleasing presentation. The lag due to this EMA is 3 bars.

```
Inputs:     Price((H+L)/2);

Vars: Smooth(0),
      Detrender(0),
      I1(0),
      Q1(0),
      Phase(0),
      DeltaPhase(0),
      InstPeriod(0),
      count(0),
      PhaseSum(0),
      Period(0);

If CurrentBar > 5 then begin
     Smooth = (4*Price + 3*Price[1] + 2*Price[2] +
     Price[3]) / 10;
     Detrender = (.0962*Smooth + .5769*Smooth[2] -
     .5769*Smooth[4] - .0962*Smooth[6])*(.075*
     Period[1] + .54);

     {Compute InPhase and Quadrature components}
     Q1 = (.0962*Detrender + .5769*Detrender[2] -
     .5769*Detrender[4] - .0962*Detrender[6])*
     (.075*Period[1] + .54);
     I1 = Detrender[3];

     {Smooth the I and Q components before applying
      the discriminator}
     I1 = .15*I1 + .85*I1[1];
     Q1 = .15*Q1 + .85*Q1[1];

     {Use ArcTangent to compute the current phase}
     If AbsValue(I1) > 0 then Phase =
     ArcTangent(AbsValue(Q1/I1));

     {Resolve the ArcTangent ambiguity for quadrants
      2, 3, and 4}
     If I1 < 0 and Q1 > 0 then Phase = 180 - Phase;
     If I1 < 0 and Q1 < 0 then Phase = 180 + Phase;
     If I1 > 0 and Q1 < 0 then Phase = 360 - Phase;
                                        (continued)
```

Figure 7.1.   Phase Accumulator cycle period measurement.

```
{Compute a differential phase, resolve phase
   wraparound from quadrant 1 to quadrant 4, and
   limit delta phase errors}
DeltaPhase = Phase[1] - Phase;
If Phase[1] < 90 and Phase > 270 then DeltaPhase
   = 360 + Phase[1] - Phase;
{Limit DeltaPhase to be within the bounds of 6
   bar and 50 bar cycles}
If DeltaPhase < 7 then DeltaPhase = 7;
If DeltaPhase > 60 then Deltaphase = 60;

{Sum DeltaPhases to reach 360 degrees. The sum is
   the instantaneous period.}
InstPeriod = 0;
PhaseSum = 0;
For count = 0 to 40 begin
        PhaseSum = PhaseSum + DeltaPhase[count];
        If PhaseSum > 360 and InstPeriod = 0 then
          begin
                InstPeriod = count;
        End;
End;

{Resolve Instantaneous Period errors and smooth}
If InstPeriod = 0 then InstPeriod =
   InstPeriod[1];
Period = .25*InstPeriod + .75*Period[1];

Plot1(Period, "DC");

End;
```

Figure 7.1. *(Continued)*.

Total lag through the Phase Accumulation cycle period
measurement consists of 6 bars for the first EMA, 3 bars for the
display smoothing EMA, 7-bars lag to compute the original
InPhase and Quadrature components, and one full cycle of this
accumulation process. Therefore, the total lag is 16 bars plus one
full-cycle period. Since the dominant cycle period is a relatively
slow varying function of time, this lag may be acceptable in
many applications.

Homodyne Discriminator

Homodyne means we are multiplying the signal by itself. More precise, we want to multiply the signal of the current bar with the complex conjugate of the signal 1 bar ago. The *complex conjugate* is, by definition, a complex number whose sign of the imaginary component has been reversed. Expressing the signal in polar coordinates, the arithmetic is

$$(\rho e^{j\omega t_n})(\rho e^{-j\omega t_{n-1}}) = \rho^2 s^{j\omega(t_n - t_{n-1})} = \rho^2 e^{j\omega}$$

The interesting result is that we get both the square of the signal amplitude and the angular frequency (2π / Period) from the product because the difference in time between samples ($t_n - t_{n-1}$) is just 1 bar. In principle, this means that we can get the instantaneous cycle period in just two successive samples. The added benefit is that we also get the square of the signal amplitude. The calculations are carried out using the real and imaginary components rather than converting them to polar coordinates. Either way, the results are the same.

The EasyLanguage code for the Homodyne Discriminator is described with reference to Figure 7.2. The InPhase and Quadrature components are computed using the Hilbert Transformer as explained in Chapter 6. These components are smoothed in a unique complex averager and then smoothed by an EMA to avoid any undesired cross products in the multiplication step that follows. Consider the result as a composite of signal and noise represented by ($S + N$). If we were to multiply this by itself, we would get $S^2 + N^2 + SN + NS$. Of the four products, three are undesired due to noise. Therefore, we must take every measure to remove undesired components prior to any multiplication. The complex averaging consists of applying the Hilbert Transformer to both the InPhase and Quadrature components. This advances the phase of each component by 90 degrees. When the InPhase component is advanced by 90 degrees, it becomes equal to the Quadrature component. Similarly, when the Quadrature component is advanced in phase by 90 degrees, it becomes the same as the negative InPhase component. So, if we perform a Hilbert Transform on an InPhase component, it will be aligned

```
Inputs:     Price((H+L)/2);

Vars: Smooth(0),
      Detrender(0),
      I1(0),
      Q1(0),
      jI(0),
      jQ(0),
      I2(0),
      Q2(0),
      Re(0),
      Im(0),
      Period(0),
      SmoothPeriod(0);

If CurrentBar > 5 then begin
    Smooth = (4*Price + 3*Price[1] + 2*Price[2] +
      Price[3]) / 10;
    Detrender = (.0962*Smooth + .5769*Smooth[2] -
      .5769*Smooth[4] - .0962*Smooth[6])*(.075*
      Period[1] + .54);

    {Compute InPhase and Quadrature components}
    Q1 = (.0962*Detrender + .5769*Detrender[2] -
      .5769*Detrender[4] - .0962*Detrender[6])*(.075*
      Period[1] + .54);
    I1 = Detrender[3];

    {Advance the phase of I1 and Q1 by 90 degrees}
    jI = (.0962*I1 + .5769*I1[2] - .5769*I1[4] -
      .0962*I1[6])*(.075*Period[1] + .54);
    jQ = (.0962*Q1 + .5769*Q1[2] - .5769*Q1[4] -
      .0962*Q1[6])*(.075*Period[1] + .54);

    {Phasor addition for 3 bar averaging)}
    I2 = I1 - jQ;
    Q2 = Q1 + jI;

    {Smooth the I and Q components before applying
      the discriminator}
                                        (continued)
```

Figure 7.2.   Homodyne Discriminator cycle period measurement.

```
        I2 = .2*I2 + .8*I2[1];
        Q2 = .2*Q2 + .8*Q2[1];

        {Homodyne Discriminator}
        Re = I2*I2[1] + Q2*Q2[1];
        Im = I2*Q2[1] - Q2*I2[1];
        Re = .2*Re + .8*Re[1];
        Im = .2*Im + .8*Im[1];
        If Im <> 0 and Re <> 0 then Period = 360/
          ArcTangent(Im/Re);
        If Period > 1.5*Period[1] then Period =
          1.5*Period[1];
        If Period < .67*Period[1] then Period =
          .67*Period[1];
        If Period < 6 then Period = 6;
        If Period > 50 then Period = 50;
        Period = .2*Period + .8*Period[1];
        SmoothPeriod = .33*Period + .67*SmoothPeriod[1];

        Plot1(SmoothPeriod, "DC");

End;
```

Figure 7.2. *(Continued).*

in phase with the Quadrature component. However, the Hilbert Transform has a 3-bar lag. The transformed InPhase component summed with the Quadrature component is therefore the mathematical equivalent of the simple average of a signal with the signal 3 bars ago. The same process applies to performing a Hilbert Transform on the imaginary component and adding it to the InPhase component. The net result is that the net complex averaging lag is 1.5 bars. After smoothing, the signal is multiplied by the complex conjugate of the signal 1 bar ago. The resulting output real component is the product of the two real components added to the product of the two imaginary components. Similarly, the resulting output imaginary component is the difference of the two input cross products. Both the real and imaginary output products are smoothed again before the cycle period is computed. This is done by taking the arctangent of the

ratio of the output imaginary component to the real component.
The rate change of the cycle period is limited to be ±50 percent
of the previous cycle period, and the resultant period is further
limited to be greater than 6 bars and less than 50 bars. Finally,
the period is smoothed for a pleasing display.

Total lag through the Homodyne Discriminator cycle period
measurement consists of the following: seven-bars lag to compute the original InPhase and Quadrature components and
4-bars lag in each of the three EMAs, and 1.5 bars for the complex averaging. Therefore, the total lag is a constant 20.5 bars.
The net smoothing is the same regardless of the measured
period. Therefore, the Signal-to-Noise Ratio as well as the lag is
constant for all cycle periods.

Dual Differentiator

We have seen how the phase angle is computed from a complex
signal as the arctangent of the ratio of the imaginary component
to the real component. Furthermore, we have seen that angular
frequency is defined as the rate change of phase. We can use
these facts to derive still a third way of using complex signals to
measure the cycle period. From the definition of the derivative
of an arctangent, the mathematics of this process are

$$\theta = \arctan\left(\frac{Q}{I}\right)$$

$$\omega = \frac{d\theta}{dt} = \frac{1}{1 + \left(\frac{Q}{I}\right)^2} \frac{(I\Delta Q - Q\Delta I)}{I^2} = \frac{(I\Delta Q - Q\Delta I)}{I^2 + Q^2}$$

Simplifying, and solving for the cycle period instead of frequency, we obtain

$$\text{Period} = \frac{2\pi(I^2 + Q^2)}{(I\Delta Q - Q\Delta I)}$$

The EasyLanguage code for the Dual Differentiator Discriminator is described with reference to Figure 7.3. The InPhase

```
Inputs:     Price((H+L)/2);

Vars: Smooth(0),
      Detrender(0),
      I1(0),
      Q1(0),
      jI(0),
      jQ(0),
      I2(0),
      Q2(0),
      Period(0),
      SmoothPeriod(0);

If CurrentBar > 5 then begin
     Smooth = (4*Price + 3*Price[1] + 2*Price[2] +
     Price[3]) / 10;
     Detrender = (.0962*Smooth + .5769*Smooth[2] -
     .5769*Smooth[4] - .0962*Smooth[6])*(.075*
     Period[1] + .54);

     {Compute InPhase and Quadrature components}
     Q1 = (.0962*Detrender + .5769*Detrender[2] -
     .5769*Detrender[4] - .0962*Detrender[6])*(.075*
     Period[1] + .54);
     I1 = Detrender[3];

     {Advance the phase of I1 and Q1 by 90 degrees}
     jI = (.0962*I1 + .5769*I1[2] - .5769*I1[4] -
     .0962*I1[6])*(.075*Period[1] + .54);
     jQ = (.0962*Q1 + .5769*Q1[2] - .5769*Q1[4] -
     .0962*Q1[6])*(.075*Period[1] + .54);

     {Phasor addition for 3 bar averaging)}
     I2 = I1 - jQ;
     Q2 = Q1 + jI;

     {Smooth the I and Q components before applying
      the discriminator}
     I2 = .15*I2 + .75*I2[1];
     Q2 = .15*Q2 + .75*Q2[1];
                                           (continued)
```

Figure 7.3. Dual Differential cycle period measurement.

```
{Dual Differential Discriminator}
Value1 = Q2*(I2 - I2[1]) - I2*(Q2 - Q2[1]);
If Value1 > .01 then Period = 6.2832*(I2*I2 +
  Q2*Q2) / Value1;
If Period > 1.5*Period[1] then Period =
  1.5*Period[1];
If Period < .67*Period[1] then Period =
  .67*Period[1];
If Period < 6 then Period = 6;
If Period > 50 then Period = 50;
Period = .15*Period + .85*Period[1];
SmoothPeriod = .33*Period + .67*SmoothPeriod[1];

Plot1(SmoothPeriod, "DC");

End;
```

Figure 7.3. *(Continued).*

and Quadrature components are computed with the Hilbert Transformer using procedures identical to those in the Dual Differentiator. These components undergo a complex averaging and are smoothed in an EMA to avoid any undesired cross products in the multiplication step that follows. The period is solved directly from the smoothed InPhase and Quadrature components. The interim calculation for the denominator is performed as Value1 to ensure that the denominator will not have a zero value. The sign of Value1 is reversed relative to the theoretical equation because the differences are looking backward in time. The rate change of the cycle period is limited to be ±50 percent of the previous cycle period, and the resultant period is further limited to be greater than 6 bars and less than 50 bars. Finally, the period is smoothed for a pleasing display.

Total lag through the Dual Differentiator Discriminator cycle period measurement consists of 7-bars lag to compute the original InPhase and Quadrature components and 4-bars lag in each of the two EMAs, plus 1.5 bars for the complex averaging. Therefore, the total lag is a constant 16.5 bars. The net smoothing is the same regardless of the measured period. Therefore, the Signal-to-Noise Ratio, as well as the lag, is constant for all cycle periods.

Cycle Measurement Comparison

We now have three techniques to measure cycle periods using complex arithmetic. We only know that they vary in lag and that the lag is relatively long in each case. The only way to determine the best technique is to exercise them in a variety of tests. The first test is designed to see how accurately the cycle measurement is made using a perfect sine wave. In Figure 7.4, we have created an analytic waveform as a pure cycle whose period increases linearly from 10 to 40 bars across the screen. The cycle length measurements of the three techniques are plotted in the first subgraph. This subgraph is scaled from 10 to 40 bars, so vertical displacement shows the measured cycle period.

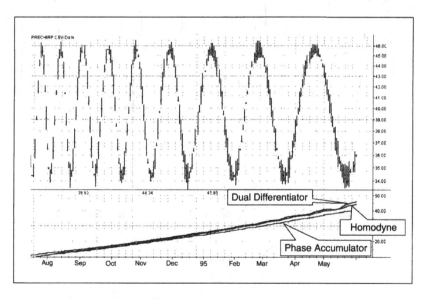

Figure 7.4.   Cycle period measurements in response to a chirped analytic waveform.

Chart created with TradeStation2000i® by Omega Research, Inc.

At first glance, it appears that the Phase Accumulator method is less accurate than the others. However, recalling that its lag is longer than the others for longer cycle periods, this apparent inaccuracy is due solely to the lag associated with the changing waveform period.

The next stress test for the cycle period measurers deciphers how rapidly the cycle measurements respond to an instantaneous shift of frequency in the analytic waveform. To do this, we created a waveform that alternately switches between a period of 15 bars and a period of 30 bars. The response of the three cycle period measurers is shown in Figure 7.5. Now we can see some differences. As expected, the Phase Accumulator is the slowest to respond to this step in the cycle period because of the

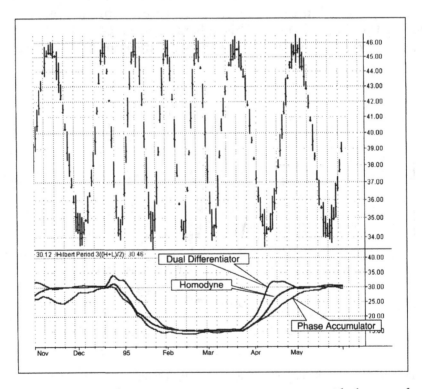

Figure 7.5. Cycle measurer transient responses to rapid changes of cycle period.

Chart created with TradeStation2000i® by Omega Research, Inc.

additional smoothing. Also as expected, the Dual Differentiator reacts the fastest in this test. However, the Dual Differentiator exhibits some overshoot error. As a result, it appears that the Homodyne approach has the superior transient response.

Another significant test finds how the cycle period measurers perform as the Signal-to-Noise Ratio degenerates. Market data almost always have a poor Signal-to-Noise Ratio, and the ability to make accurate measurements is crucial. In fact, it was this stress test that led to additional smoothing prior to the multiplication operations in the Homodyne and Dual Differentiator cycle period measurers. Without this smoothing, the performance in low Signal-to-Noise environments was just awful, producing measured cycle periods nearly half the correct period. The performance of the cycle period measurers are compared in Figure 7.6 as a function of Signal-to-Noise Ratio when measuring a theoretical twenty-bar sinewave signal. It is clear from Figure 7.6 that the Homodyne approach is not only more accurate at high Signal-to-Noise Ratios but its performance degrades more gracefully as the noise is increased relative to the signal strength.

The real acid test of the cycle period measurers' performance determines how well they do when acting on real data. We do this in Figure 7.7. All three tend to give similar measurements

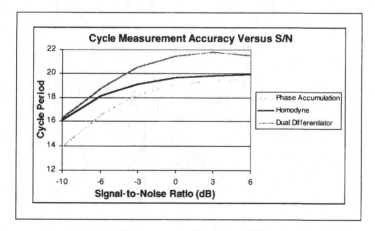

Figure 7.6. Phase measurer performance as a function of Signal-to-Noise Ratio.

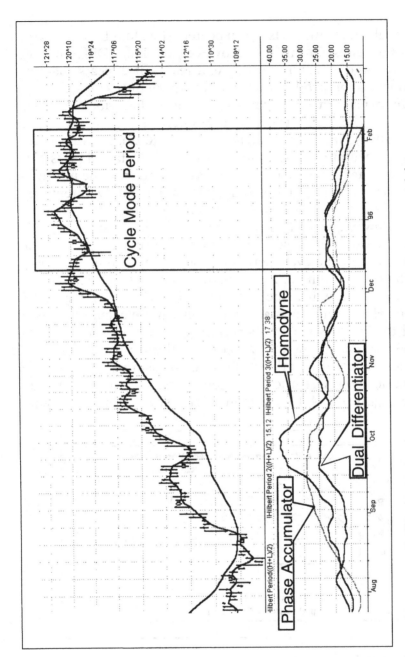

Figure 7.7. Three cycle performance measurements on real data.
Chart created with TradeStation2000i® by Omega Research, Inc.

when the market is in a Cycle Mode. However, there is a wide difference in the measurements when the market is in a Trend Mode. My observations have led me to conclude that the Homodyne is overall more accurate in measurement of cycles when the market is in a Trend Mode.

For all these reasons I conclude that the Homodyne Discriminator is the superior approach. This frequency measurer is used throughout the remainder of this book.

Key Points to Remember

- A basic definition of a cycle is a constant rate change of phase.
- The Hilbert Transform generates InPhase and Quadrature components from which the phase at each bar can be measured.
- The phase rate of change is established as the differential phase from bar to bar.
- Complex averaging can be accomplished by applying the Hilbert Transformer to both the InPhase and Quadrature components, advancing their phase by 90 degrees. The phase-advanced components are then algebraically added to their orthogonal counterparts to effect the averaging.
- There are at least three different ways to measure cycle period using the InPhase and Quadrature components.
- The Homodyne Discriminator is the superior cycle period measurer.

Chapter 8

SIGNAL-TO-NOISE RATIO

*Logic is a system whereby one may
go wrong with confidence.*

—Charles Kettering

The *signal amplitude* is simply the length of the phasor. Recalling the Pythagorean Theorem, the length of the phasor is the square root of the sum of the squares of the InPhase and Quadrature components. We therefore have the signal amplitude on a bar-by-bar basis after we take the Hilbert Transform.

The signal amplitude is not of much use by itself. However, if we can estimate the signal amplitude relative to the market noise, we then have a tool that estimates the quality of our technical analysis. With the kind of market data now available, let us develop a unique definition of noise. A sampled signal is shown in Figure 8.1(*a*) as a sine wave with the sampling uncertainty represented as the high and low of each bar. The high and low is the uncertainty of each of our perfect sinewave sample points. We can make good trades as long as our signal amplitude is much larger than the average daily range of the bars. Another case for the same signal amplitude is shown in Figure 8.1(*b*). When half the average daily range becomes equal to the signal amplitude, making money on a trade becomes a crapshoot. Under this condition, it is possible to make an entry at the low of the bar (which contains the signal high) and make an exit at the high of the bar (which contains the signal low) for zero profit. We will therefore term the case where half the average daily

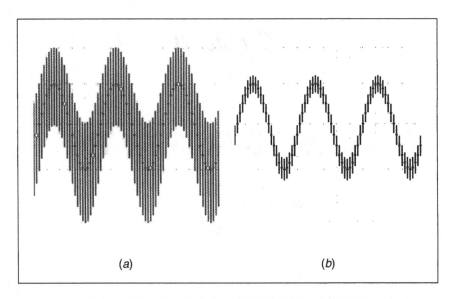

Figure 8.1.   (a) Fourteen dB SNR. (b) Zero dB SNR.

trading range is equal to the signal amplitude as our zero decibel Signal-to-Noise Ratio (0 dB SNR) condition. We want the signal amplitude to be at least twice the noise amplitude (6 dB SNR) so that there exists a reasonable chance to make a profit from our analysis.

We can define the *noise* as a smoothed average of the daily trading range. We can tolerate a 9-bar lag to compute such an average because the range tends not to change much, and so the noise will be an Exponential Moving Average (EMA) with an alpha of 0.1. The trading range is simply the high minus the low of each bar. The EasyLanguage code to compute the SNR is given in Figure 8.2. This code is almost identical to the one we use for the Homodyne Discriminator with a few additions. First, the noise is computed as the variable "Range" near the top of the code. Second, the signal power is computed by adding the square of the InPhase component to the square of the Quadrature component.

The SNR in decibels is calculated in a single line of code near the end. The signal power is divided by the noise power to get a power ratio. The value in decibels is computed as 10 times the

```
Inputs:     Price((H+L)/2);

Vars: Range(0),
      Smooth(0),
      Detrender(0),
      I1(0),
      Q1(0),
      jI(0),
      jQ(0),
      I2(0),
      Q2(0),
      Re(0),
      Im(0),
      Period(0),
      SmoothPeriod(0),
      SNR(0);

If CurrentBar > 5 then begin

      {Compute "Noise" as the average range}
      Range = .1*(H - L) + .9*Range[1];

      Smooth = (4*Price + 3*Price[1] + 2*Price[2] +
        Price[3]) / 10;
      Detrender = (.0962*Smooth + .5769*Smooth[2] -
        .5769*Smooth[4] - .0962*Smooth[6])*(.075*
        Period[1] + .54);

      {Compute InPhase and Quadrature components}
      Q1 = (.0962*Detrender + .5769*Detrender[2] -
        .5769*Detrender[4] - .0962*Detrender[6])*
        (.075*Period[1] + .54);
      I1 = Detrender[3];

      {Advance the phase of I1 and Q1 by 90 degrees}
      jI = (.0962*I1 + .5769*I1[2] - .5769*I1[4] -
        .0962*I1[6])*(.075*Period[1] + .54);
      jQ = (.0962*Q1 + .5769*Q1[2] - .5769*Q1[4] -
        .0962*Q1[6])*(.075*Period[1] + .54);
                                        (continued)
```

Figure 8.2. Computing the SNR.

```
{Phasor addition for 3 bar averaging}
I2 = I1 - jQ;
Q2 = Q1 + jI;

{Smooth the I and Q components before applying
  the discriminator}
I2 = .2*I2 + .8*I2[1];
Q2 = .2*Q2 + .8*Q2[1];

{Homodyne Discriminator}
Re = I2*I2[1] + Q2*Q2[1];
Im = I2*Q2[1] - Q2*I2[1];
Re = .2*Re + .8*Re[1];
Im = .2*Im + .8*Im[1];
If Im <> 0 and Re <> 0 then Period =
  360/ArcTangent(Im/Re);
If Period > 1.5*Period[1] then Period =
  1.5*Period[1];
If Period < .67*Period[1] then Period =
  .67*Period[1];
If Period < 6 then Period = 6;
If Period > 50 then Period = 50;
Period = .2*Period + .8*Period[1];

{Compute smoothed SNR in Decibels, guarding
  against a divide by zero error}
If Range > 0 then SNR = .25*(10*Log((I1*I1 +
  Q1*Q1)/(Range*Range))/Log(10) + 6) +
  .75*SNR[1];

{Plot Results}
Plot1(SNR, "SNR");
Plot2(6, "Ref");

End;
```

Figure 8.2.   (*Continued*).

logarithm of the power ratio. Since EasyLanguage takes only natural logarithms, the logarithm must be converted to log base 10 by being divided by the natural logarithm of 10. A compensating term of 6 dB must be added due to our definition of signal to noise. As defined earlier, the signal amplitude is the length of the phasor. At 0 dB, the peak-to-peak noise signal is twice the amplitude of the signal. Therefore, when we compute the 0 dB case, the ratio is calculated to be 10*Log(1/2)^2 = –6 dB. We must then add 6 dB back into the computation to remove this bias, establishing our definition of 0 dB SNR.

Assuming the noise is relatively constant, the lag of the Signal-to-Noise Indicator is just the 7 bars that result from the Hilbert Transformer plus the 3 bars due to smoothing of the display.

There is another way to compute the SNR. Recall that in the derivation of the Homodyne Discriminator, the amplitude squared fell out of the equation automatically when we solved for the frequency. In EasyLanguage code, the amplitude squared is the sum of the variables Re and Im. Therefore, our alternate solution for the SNR is obtained by replacing (I1*I1 + Q1*Q1) with (Re + Im). That is the only change in the code shown in Figure 8.3. The alternate calculation uses the signal information that is smoothed by two EMAs, causing a 3-bar lag each, plus the lag induced by the complex averaging of 1.5 bars. Therefore, we expect the alternate SNR computation to produce a result that is smoother and has an additional 7.5-bar lag as compared to the first (or, primary) calculation. The two SNR computations are compared in Figure 8.4. Our expectation of a smoother and more delayed alternate computation is manifest.

The 10-bar lag induced by the computation of the Primary SNR makes this calculation unusable for practical trading. The additional lag of the Alternate SNR makes its use unthinkable. By carefully examining the required conditions, we can arrive at an SNR Indicator that has an acceptable lag.

The first condition of the Hilbert Transform is that its transfer response must have a zero transfer response at zero frequency. That means the signal must be detrended. The first thing we do after the initial smoothing is to use the Detrender as the Quadra-

```
Inputs:     Price((H+L)/2);

Vars: Range(0),
      Smooth(0),
      Detrender(0),
      I1(0),
      Q1(0),
      jI(0),
      jQ(0),
      I2(0),
      Q2(0),
      Re(0),
      Im(0),
      Period(0),
      SmoothPeriod(0),
      SNR(0);

If CurrentBar > 5 then begin

      {Compute "Noise" as the average range}
      Range = .1*(H - L) + .9*Range[1];

      Smooth = (4*Price + 3*Price[1] + 2*Price[2] +
        Price[3]) / 10;
      Detrender = (.0962*Smooth + .5769*Smooth[2] -
        .5769*Smooth[4] - .0962*Smooth[6])*(.075*
        Period[1] + .54);

      {Compute InPhase and Quadrature components}
      Q1 = (.0962*Detrender + .5769*Detrender[2] -
        .5769*Detrender[4] - .0962*Detrender[6])*(.075*
        Period[1] + .54);
      I1 = Detrender[3];

      {Advance the phase of I1 and Q1 by 90 degrees}
      jI = (.0962*I1 + .5769*I1[2] - .5769*I1[4] -
        .0962*I1[6])*(.075*Period[1] + .54);
      jQ = (.0962*Q1 + .5769*Q1[2] - .5769*Q1[4] -
        .0962*Q1[6])*(.075*Period[1] + .54);

      {Phasor addition for 3 bar averaging)}
                                      (continued)
```

Figure 8.3. Alternate SNR computation.

```
I2 = I1 - jQ;
Q2 = Q1 + jI;

{Smooth the I and Q components before applying
  the discriminator}
I2 = .2*I2 + .8*I2[1];
Q2 = .2*Q2 + .8*Q2[1];

{Homodyne Discriminator}
Re = I2*I2[1] + Q2*Q2[1];
Im = I2*Q2[1] - Q2*I2[1];
Re = .2*Re + .8*Re[1];
Im = .2*Im + .8*Im[1];
If Im <> 0 and Re <> 0 then Period =
  360/ArcTangent(Im/Re);
If Period > 1.5*Period[1] then Period =
  1.5*Period[1];
If Period < .67*Period[1] then Period =
  .67*Period[1];
If Period < 6 then Period = 6;
If Period > 50 then Period = 50;
Period = .2*Period + .8*Period[1];

{Compute smoothed SNR in Decibels, guarding
  against a divide by zero error}
If Range > 0 then SNR = .25*(10*Log((Re +
  Im)/(Range*Range))/Log(10) + 6) + .75*SNR[1];

{Plot Results}
Plot1(SNR, "SNR");
Plot2(6, "Ref");

End;
```

Figure 8.3. (*Continued*).

ture component of the Hilbert Transform. If we shorten the Detrender to a 2-bar momentum, the resulting lag is only 1 bar. Because of the shorter momentum, we need a more aggressive amplitude correction as a function of the measured period. We can measure slowly varying periods as we have done previously before proceeding with the calculation of the SNR. We also know that if

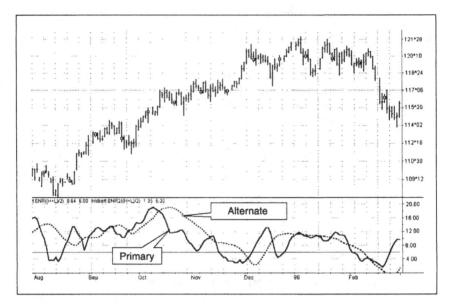

Figure 8.4.   The alternate SNR computation is smoother and has more lag than the primary computation.

Chart created with TradeStation2000i ® by Omega Research, Inc.

we take a Simple Moving Average (SMA) over half the measured period, the lag of this average is a quarter cycle. A quarter cycle is 90 degrees of phase lag—exactly the lag needed to create the InPhase component from the Quadrature component. This filtering also reduces the dominant cycle amplitude by $2/\pi$, so an additional $\pi/2$ amplitude correction term must be included in the computation of the InPhase component.

All these conditions have been included in the computation of the Enhanced SNR Indicator, as described in the code of Figure 8.5. In this code, the period of the measured dominant cycle is calculated in exactly the same manner as we calculated it for the Primary SNR Indicator. Near the end of the code, after the dominant cycle is determined, we compute the SNR. The Quadrature component Q3 is calculated by multiplying the 2-bar momentum of the Weighted Moving Average (WMA) smoothing by the dominant cycle amplitude correction factor. The correction terms were derived by observing the output amplitude of the 2-bar momen-

```
{*********************************************************
Description : Enhanced Signal to Noise Ratio Indicator
*********************************************************}

Inputs:     Price((H+L)/2);

Vars: Smooth(0),
      Detrender(0),
      I1(0),
      Q1(0),
      jI(0),
      jQ(0),
      I2(0),
      Q2(0),
      Re(0),
      Im(0),
      Period(0),
      SmoothPeriod(0),
      count(0),
      I3(0),
      Q3(0),
      Signal(0),
      Noise(0),
      SNR(0);

If CurrentBar > 5 then begin
    Smooth = (4*Price + 3*Price[1] + 2*Price[2] +
      Price[3]) / 10;
    Detrender = (.0962*Smooth + .5769*Smooth[2] -
      .5769*Smooth[4] - .0962*Smooth[6])*(.075*
      Period[1] + .54);

    {Compute InPhase and Quadrature components}
    Q1 = (.0962*Detrender + .5769*Detrender[2] -
      .5769*Detrender[4] - .0962*Detrender[6])*
      (.075*Period[1] + .54);
    I1 = Detrender[3];

    {Advance the phase of I1 and Q1 by 90 degrees}
    jI = (.0962*I1 + .5769*I1[2] - .5769*I1[4] -
      .0962*I1[6])*(.075*Period[1] + .54);
    jQ = (.0962*Q1 + .5769*Q1[2] - .5769*Q1[4] -
      .0962*Q1[6])*(.075*Period[1] + .54);
                                        (continued)
```

Figure 8.5. Enhanced SNR computation.

87

```
{Phasor addition for 3 bar averaging)}
I2 = I1 - jQ;
Q2 = Q1 + jI;

{Smooth the I and Q components before applying
  the discriminator}
I2 = .2*I2 + .8*I2[1];
Q2 = .2*Q2 + .8*Q2[1];

{Homodyne Discriminator}
Re = I2*I2[1] + Q2*Q2[1];
Im = I2*Q2[1] - Q2*I2[1];
Re = .2*Re + .8*Re[1];
Im = .2*Im + .8*Im[1];
If Im <> 0 and Re <> 0 then Period =
  360/ArcTangent(Im/Re);
If Period > 1.5*Period[1] then Period =
  1.5*Period[1];
If Period < .67*Period[1] then Period =
  .67*Period[1];
If Period < 6 then Period = 6;
If Period > 50 then Period = 50;
Period = .2*Period + .8*Period[1];
SmoothPeriod = .33*Period + .67*SmoothPeriod[1];

Q3 = .5*(Smooth - Smooth[2])*(.1759*SmoothPeriod +
  .4607);
I3 = 0;
For count = 0 to Int(SmoothPeriod/2) - 1 begin
      I3 = I3 + Q3[count];
End;
I3 = 1.57*I3 / Int(SmoothPeriod/2);

Signal = I3*I3 + Q3*Q3;
Noise = .1*(H - L)*(H - L)*.25 + .9*Noise[1];
If (Noise <> 0 and Signal <> 0) then SNR =
  .33*(10*Log(Signal/Noise)/Log(10)) + .67*SNR[1];

Plot1(SNR, "SNR");
Plot2(6, "Ref");

end;
```

Figure 8.5. *(Continued).*

tum when the chirp waveform of Figure 7.4 was applied. The output amplitudes for the 10-bar cycle period and the 40-bar cycle period were used to compute the straight line compensation terms 0.1759 and 0.4607. The InPhase component I3 is computed as the half-dominant cycle moving average multiplied by the $\pi/2$ amplitude correction term. Again, the noise power is computed as the square of the averaged range of the bars, and the signal power is computed as the sum of the square of the InPhase component and the square of the Quadrature component. The total lag of the Enhanced SNR Indicator is only 4 bars, compared to the 10-bar lag of the Primary SNR Indicator. This lag comprises 1 bar for the initial smoothing, 1 bar for the computation of the Quadrature component, and 2 bars for the final smoothing of the indicator.

The performance of the Enhanced SNR Indicator is shown in Figure 8.6 with the same data that we used in the computation of the Primary and Alternate SNR Indicators in Figure 8.4. The Enhanced SNR Indicator now has lag properties that make it useful for trading.

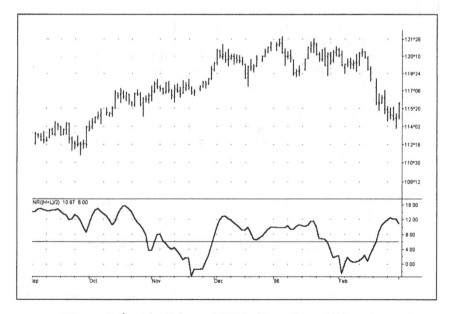

Figure 8.6. The Enhanced SNR Indicator has minimum lag.
Chart created with TradeStation2000i ® by Omega Research, Inc.

```
{*********************************************************
Description : Hilbert Oscillator
*********************************************************}

Inputs:     Price((H+L)/2);

Vars: Smooth(0),
      Detrender(0),
      I1(0),
      Q1(0),
      jI(0),
      jQ(0),
      I2(0),
      Q2(0),
      Re(0),
      Im(0),
      Period(0),
      SmoothPeriod(0),
      count(0),
      I3(0),
      Q3(0);

If CurrentBar > 5 then begin
      Smooth = (4*Price + 3*Price[1] + 2*Price[2] +
        Price[3]) / 10;
      Detrender = (.0962*Smooth + .5769*Smooth[2] -
        .5769*Smooth[4] - .0962*Smooth[6])*(.075*
        Period[1] + .54);

      {Compute InPhase and Quadrature components}
      Q1 = (.0962*Detrender + .5769*Detrender[2] -
        .5769*Detrender[4] - .0962*Detrender[6])*
        (.075*Period[1] + .54);
      I1 = Detrender[3];

      {Advance the phase of I1 and Q1 by 90 degrees}
      jI = (.0962*I1 + .5769*I1[2] - .5769*I1[4] -
        .0962*I1[6])*(.075*Period[1] + .54);
      jQ = (.0962*Q1 + .5769*Q1[2] - .5769*Q1[4] -
        .0962*Q1[6])*(.075*Period[1] + .54);
                                             (continued)
```

Figure 8.7. Hilbert Oscillator computation.

```
        {Phasor addition for 3 bar averaging)}
        I2 = I1 - jQ;
        Q2 = Q1 + jI;

        {Smooth the I and Q components before applying
          the discriminator}
        I2 = .2*I2 + .8*I2[1];
        Q2 = .2*Q2 + .8*Q2[1];

        {Homodyne Discriminator}
        Re = I2*I2[1] + Q2*Q2[1];
        Im = I2*Q2[1] - Q2*I2[1];
        Re = .2*Re + .8*Re[1];
        Im = .2*Im + .8*Im[1];
        If Im <> 0 and Re <> 0 then Period =
           360/ArcTangent(Im/Re);
        If Period > 1.5*Period[1] then Period =
           1.5*Period[1];
        If Period < .67*Period[1] then Period =
           .67*Period[1];
        If Period < 6 then Period = 6;
        If Period > 50 then Period = 50;
        Period = .2*Period + .8*Period[1];
        SmoothPeriod = .33*Period + .67*SmoothPeriod[1];

        Q3 = .5*(Smooth - Smooth[2])*(.1759*SmoothPeriod +
          .4607);
        I3 = 0;
        For count = 0 to Int(SmoothPeriod/2) - 1 begin
          I3 = I3 + Q3[count];
        End;
        I3 = 1.57*I3 / Int(SmoothPeriod/2);
        Value1 = 0;
        For count = 0 to Int(SmoothPeriod/4) - 1 begin
          Value1 = Value1 + Q3[count];
        End;
        Value1 = 1.25*Value1 / Int(SmoothPeriod/4);

        Plot1(I3, "I");
        Plot2(Value1, "IQ");

End;
```

Figure 8.7. (*Continued*).

While not related to SNR, the reduced lag procedure that leads to the Enhanced SNR Indicator suggests a way to develop a fast and responsive oscillator. If we compute a quarter-cycle moving average of Q3, it will lag Q3 by 45 degrees. The half-cycle moving average of Q3 lags Q3 by 90 degrees. Since Q3 leads the cycle component of the signal by 90 degrees, it follows that the two moving averages will cross 22.5 degrees in advance of the crests and valleys of a theoretically perfect cycle. Although this will not be a leading indicator because of the 2-bar lag required to compute Q3, it does prove itself to be superior to most currently available oscillators. The code to compute the Hilbert Oscillator is given in Figure 8.7, and its performance is shown in Figure 8.8. The bandwidth for the computation of Value1 is twice the bandwidth of I3. Therefore, the amplitude compensation will be less, approximately the square root of 1.57, which is about 1.25.

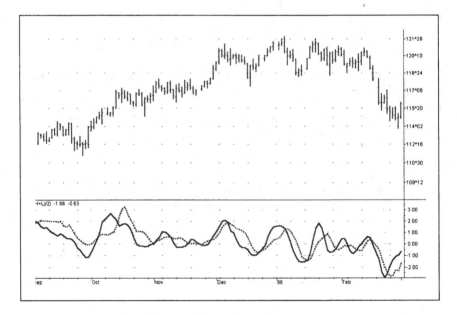

Figure 8.8.   The Hilbert Oscillator identifies every major turning point.
Chart created with TradeStation2000i® by Omega Research, Inc.

Key Points to Remember

- The average high to low range of the bars can be considered noise because the range is the uncertainty of making good Cycle Mode trades.
- The phasor amplitude is the signal amplitude.
- Cycle Mode trading should be avoided when the SNR is below 6 dB.
- The Primary SNR Indicator has a lag of 10 bars.
- The Alternate SNR Indicator has an additional 7.5 bars of lag, thus making a total lag of 17.5 bars.
- The Enhanced SNR Indicator reduces lag to only 4 bars.
- A useful oscillator results from minimizing Hilbert Transform lag.

Chapter 9

THE SINEWAVE INDICATOR

A painter can hang his pictures,
but a writer can only hang himself.

—EDWARD DAHLBERG

As noted in Chapter 6, the Hilbert Transform synthesizes the InPhase and Quadrature components from the analytic waveform. We can then immediately compute the phase of the signal by taking the arctangent of the ratio of these components. In principle, that should tell us where we are positioned within the cycle. Unfortunately, this is not true. The first problem is that the Hilbert Transform induces a lag of 7 bars. That lag is a substantial portion of most tradable cycles. The second problem is that even that phase measurement is typically very noisy, requiring many more bars of data to be used. The lag thus renders the phase measurement made directly from the Hilbert Transform unusable.

However, the Hilbert Transform can be used to measure the dominant cycle period. Since the dominant cycle period is a slowly varying function of time, the lag of this measurement is often acceptable. We assume this to be the case for our analyses. Knowing the dominant cycle period, we can heterodyne the perfect dominant cycle with the original price data. Heterodyning produces the sum and difference frequencies. Since both the price data and the dominant cycle have the same frequency, we can isolate the direct current (DC, or zero frequency) component by filtering. This process gives the phase of the dominant cycle without lag. Thus, we can compute indicators having zero lag from this information.

The EasyLanguage code to measure dominant cycle phase is described with reference to Figure 9.1. The majority of the code computes the Hilbert Transform and finds the dominant cycle period using the preferred Homodyne Discriminator. The phase computation part of the code begins with a comment line as a flag. The first step is to smooth the price data. Any components having a cycle period less than 6 bars are not desired and should be removed before the computations commence. We remove them by employing a 4-bar Weighted Moving Average (WMA). The WMA introduces 1 bar of lag that we will want to remove by compensation later in the calculations. Next, the smoothed data are multiplied by the real (cosine) component of the dominant cycle and independently by the imaginary (sine) component of the dominant cycle. The products are summed then over one full dominant cycle. We compute the phase angle as the arctangent of the ratio of the imaginary part to the real part. The phase increases from left to right across the chart. A 90-degree reference shift is immediately introduced. Next, we must remove the 1-bar lag that was introduced by the smoothing of the price. This is done by adding the phase corresponding to a 1-bar lag of the smoothed dominant cycle period.

Finally, the phase ambiguity is removed for those cases where the imaginary part is less than zero, providing a 360-degree phase presentation. Normally, we think of the phase as going from 0 to 360 degrees and then repeating for the next cycle. However, we perform the cycle wraparound at 315 degrees because there is a tendency for the phase to be near 0 degrees when the market is in a downtrend. If the wraparound were at 360 degrees, the swing from the bottom of the subgraph to the top provides less than a pleasing display.

The way the phase display behaves in a Trend Mode can potentially provide some useful information to a trader. First, phase tends to stop advancing when the market is in a Trend Mode. That is, there is no rate of change and, therefore, no cycle. The phase tends to rest near 180 degrees when the market is in an uptrend and tends to rest near 0 degrees when the market is

```
Inputs:     Price((H+L)/2);

Vars: Smooth(0),
      Detrender(0),
      I1(0),
      Q1(0),
      jI(0),
      jQ(0),
      I2(0),
      Q2(0),
      Re(0),
      Im(0),
      Period(0),
      SmoothPeriod(0),
      SmoothPrice(0),
      DCPeriod(0),
      RealPart(0),
      ImagPart(0),
      count(0),
      DCPhase(0);

If CurrentBar > 5 then begin
      Smooth = (4*Price + 3*Price[1] + 2*Price[2] +
        Price[3]) / 10;
      Detrender = (.0962*Smooth + .5769*Smooth[2] -
        .5769*Smooth[4] - .0962*Smooth[6])*(.075*
        Period[1] + .54);

      {Compute InPhase and Quadrature components}
      Q1 = (.0962*Detrender + .5769*Detrender[2] -
        .5769*Detrender[4] - .0962*Detrender[6])*(.075*
        Period[1] + .54);
      I1 = Detrender[3];

      {Advance the phase of I1 and Q1 by 90 degrees}
      jI = (.0962*I1 + .5769*I1[2] - .5769*I1[4] -
        .0962*I1[6])*(.075*Period[1] + .54);
      jQ = (.0962*Q1 + .5769*Q1[2] - .5769*Q1[4] -
        .0962*Q1[6])*(.075*Period[1] + .54);
```
                                         (continued)

Figure 9.1. Computing the dominant cycle phase.

```
{Phasor addition for 3 bar averaging)}
I2 = I1 - jQ;
Q2 = Q1 + jI;

{Smooth the I and Q components before applying
  the discriminator}
I2 = .2*I2 + .8*I2[1];
Q2 = .2*Q2 + .8*Q2[1];

{Homodyne Discriminator}
Re = I2*I2[1] + Q2*Q2[1];
Im = I2*Q2[1] - Q2*I2[1];
Re = .2*Re + .8*Re[1];
Im = .2*Im + .8*Im[1];
If Im <> 0 and Re <> 0 then Period =
  360/ArcTangent(Im/Re);
If Period > 1.5*Period[1] then Period =
  1.5*Period[1];
If Period < .67*Period[1] then Period =
  .67*Period[1];
If Period < 6 then Period = 6;
If Period > 50 then Period = 50;
Period = .2*Period + .8*Period[1];
SmoothPeriod = .33*Period + .67*SmoothPeriod[1];

{Compute Dominant Cycle Phase}
SmoothPrice = (4*Price + 3*Price[1] + 2*Price[2] +
  Price[3]) / 10;
DCPeriod = IntPortion(SmoothPeriod + .5);
RealPart = 0;
ImagPart = 0;
For count = 0 To DCPeriod - 1 begin
      RealPart = RealPart + Cosine(360 * count /
        DCPeriod) * (SmoothPrice[count]);
      ImagPart = ImagPart + Sine(360 * count /
        DCPeriod) * (SmoothPrice[count]);
End;
If AbsValue(RealPart) > 0.001 then DCPhase =
  Arctangent(ImagPart / RealPart);
If AbsValue(RealPart) <= 0.001 then DCPhase = 90 *
  Sign(ImagPart);
DCPhase = DCPhase + 90;
```
(continued)

Figure 9.1. *(Continued)*.

```
{Compensate for one bar lag of the Weighted
  Moving Average}
DCPhase = DCPhase + 360 / SmoothPeriod;

If ImagPart < 0 then DCPhase = DCPhase + 180;
If DCPhase > 315 then DCPhase = DCPhase - 360;

Plot1(DCPhase, "Phase");

End;
```

Figure 9.1. (*Continued*).

in a downtrend. The reason for this is that although the price
data have been detrended, there is still some residual trend
across the 6 bars of the Detrender. The summation of the product of the pure trend to the complex components of the dominant cycle can be thought of as similar to the integrals

$$\text{Im} = \int_0^{2\pi} x\, \text{Sin}(x)dx = -2\pi$$

$$\text{Re} = \int_0^{2\pi} x\, \text{Cos}(x)dx = 0$$

The ratio of the RealPart to the Imaginary will always be a
small number when the market is in a Trend Mode. However,
the sign of that number will be negative when the market is in
an uptrend and positive when the market is in a downtrend. As
a result, the phase will be near 180 degrees in uptrending markets and near 0 degrees in downtrending markets.

We obtain the Sinewave Indicator by plotting the sine of the
measured phase angle. This gives us an oscillator that always
swings between the limits of −1 and +1. We enhance the usabil-
ity of this oscillator by plotting the sine of the phase angle
advanced by 45 degrees. The effect of plotting these two lines is
shown for both the phasor and time-domain presentations in
Figure 9.2. Adding 45 degrees clearly advances the phasor from a

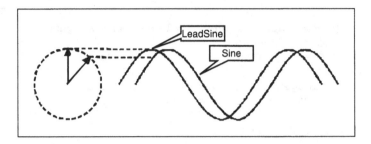

Figure 9.2. Phasor and time-domain views of the Sinewave Indicator.

45-degree slant to the vertical position. This phase advance means the LeadSine waveform will crest before the sine crests. The LeadSine and Sine lines cross 22.5 degrees, or 1/16th of a cycle, before the turning point of the cycle is reached. If the market has a cycle of 16 bars or less, this is a signal to enter or exit a trade immediately. If the market has a longer cycle, there is some built-in anticipation time before you pull the trigger.

Compared to conventional oscillators such as the Stochastic or Relative Strength Indicator (RSI), the Sinewave Indicator has two major advantages. These are

1. The Sinewave Indicator anticipates the Cycle Mode turning point rather than waiting for confirmation.
2. The phase does not advance when the market is in a Trend Mode. Therefore, the Sinewave Indicator tends to not give false whipsaw signals when the market is in a Trend Mode.

An additional advantage is that the anticipation signal is obtained strictly by mathematically advancing the phase. Momentum is not employed. Therefore, the Sinewave Indicator signals are no more noisy than the original signal.

The code to compute and display the Sinewave Indicator is given in Figure 9.3. This EasyLanguage code is identical to the code given for the phase in Figure 9.1 except for the plot statements.

The Phase and Sinewave Indicators are plotted against both theoretical analytic waveforms and real-world data to demon-

```
Inputs:     Price((H+L)/2);

Vars: Smooth(0),
      Detrender(0),
      I1(0),
      Q1(0),
      jI(0),
      jQ(0),
      I2(0),
      Q2(0),
      Re(0),
      Im(0),
      Period(0),
      SmoothPeriod(0),
      SmoothPrice(0),
      DCPeriod(0),
      RealPart(0),
      ImagPart(0),
      count(0),
      DCPhase(0);

If CurrentBar > 5 then begin
    Smooth = (4*Price + 3*Price[1] + 2*Price[2] +
      Price[3]) / 10;
    Detrender = (.0962*Smooth + .5769*Smooth[2] -
      .5769*Smooth[4] - .0962*Smooth[6])*(.075*
      Period[1] + .54);

    {Compute InPhase and Quadrature components}
    Q1 = (.0962*Detrender + .5769*Detrender[2] -
      .5769*Detrender[4] - .0962*Detrender[6])*
      (.075*Period[1] + .54);
    I1 = Detrender[3];

    {Advance the phase of I1 and Q1 by 90 degrees}
    jI = (.0962*I1 + .5769*I1[2] - .5769*I1[4] -
      .0962*I1[6])*(.075*Period[1] + .54);
    jQ = (.0962*Q1 + .5769*Q1[2] - .5769*Q1[4] -
      .0962*Q1[6])*(.075*Period[1] + .54);

    {Phasor addition for 3 bar averaging}
    I2 = I1 - jQ;
    Q2 = Q1 + jI;
```
(continued)

Figure 9.3.   EasyLanguage code to compute the Sinewave Indicator.

```
{Smooth the I and Q components before applying
  the discriminator}
I2 = .2*I2 + .8*I2[1];
Q2 = .2*Q2 + .8*Q2[1];

{Homodyne Discriminator}
Re = I2*I2[1] + Q2*Q2[1];
Im = I2*Q2[1] - Q2*I2[1];
Re = .2*Re + .8*Re[1];
Im = .2*Im + .8*Im[1];
If Im <> 0 and Re <> 0 then Period =
  360/ArcTangent (Im/Re);
If Period > 1.5*Period[1] then Period =
  1.5*Period[1];
If Period < .67*Period[1] then Period =
  .67*Period[1];
If Period < 6 then Period = 6;
If Period > 50 then Period = 50;
Period = .2*Period + .8*Period[1];
SmoothPeriod = .33*Period + .67*SmoothPeriod[1];

{Compute Dominant Cycle Phase}
SmoothPrice = (4*Price + 3*Price[1] + 2*Price[2] +
  Price[3]) / 10;
DCPeriod = IntPortion(SmoothPeriod + .5);
RealPart = 0;
ImagPart = 0;
For count = 0 To DCPeriod - 1 begin
      RealPart = RealPart + Cosine(360 * count /
        DCPeriod) * (SmoothPrice[count]);
      ImagPart = ImagPart + Sine(360 * count /
        DCPeriod) * (SmoothPrice[count]);
End;
If AbsValue(RealPart) > 0.001 then DCPhase =
  Arctangent(ImagPart / RealPart);
If AbsValue(RealPart) <= 0.001 then DCPhase = 90 *
  Sign(ImagPart);
DCPhase = DCPhase + 90;
```
                                            (continued)

Figure 9.3. *(Continued)*.

```
{Compensate for one bar lag of the Weighted
   Moving Average}
DCPhase = DCPhase + 360 / SmoothPeriod;

If ImagPart < 0 then DCPhase = DCPhase + 180;
If DCPhase > 315 then DCPhase = DCPhase - 360;

Plot1(Sine(DCPhase), "Sine");
Plot2(Sine(DCPhase + 45), "LeadSine");

End;
```

Figure 9.3. (*Continued*).

strate their performance. Figure 9.4 shows a theoretical sinewave analytic waveform whose period increases linearly from 10 to 40 bars. The Sinewave and Phase Indicators are displayed in the two subgraphs. Note how the phase rate of change decreases as the cycle period becomes longer. The dotted line is a typical point of reference, illustrating that the analytic waveform and the Sine line of the Sinewave Indicator crest simultaneously, and the measured phase is 90 degrees at this point. The LeadSine always crosses the Sine line before the turning point in the cycle, giving advance indication of the cyclic turning point. The amount of advance warning relative to the length of the cycle is less for the shorter cycles.

A real-world trading scenario is depicted in Figure 9.5. The market is in a Trend Mode for nearly the entire left half of the chart, as identified by the lack of phase rate of change and lack of crossovers by the Sinewave Indicator. The Cycle Mode of the chart is identified by the rectangle. The Cycle Mode starts when the phase rate of change is approximately the same as the phase rate of change of the dominant cycle. The Cycle Mode ends when the phase rate of change becomes negative—a clear impossibility. During the Cycle Mode period, the Sinewave Indicator gives three buy signals and two sell signals. All are excellent except the last one, which almost always happens when the cycle fails.

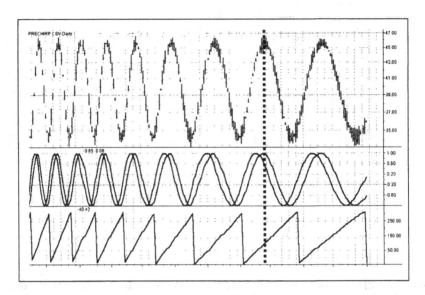

Figure 9.4. The Sinewave Indicator always gives an advanced turning-point warning.
Chart created with TradeStation2000i ® by Omega Research, Inc.

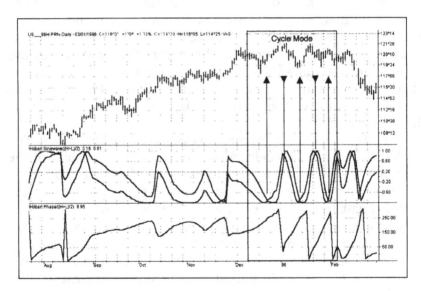

Figure 9.5. The Sinewave Indicator gives correct Cycle Mode signals.
Chart created with TradeStation2000i ® by Omega Research, Inc.

Key Points to Remember

- The phase computed from the Hilbert Transform cannot be used directly because of the lag that results from computing.
- The cycle period measurement is a slowly varying function of time and may be used as the dominant cycle.
- The phase of the dominant cycle is computed by heterodyning the complex dominant cycle with the smoothed analytic waveform and taking the arctangent of the complex components.
- The phase hovers near 0 degrees in downtrends and near 180 degrees in uptrends.
- The Sinewave Indicator consists of the Sine of the Dominant Cycle phase and the Sine of the Dominant Cycle phase advanced by 45 degrees (LeadSine).
- The Sinewave Indicator gives entry and exit signals 1/16th of a cycle period in advance of the cycle turning point.
- The Sinewave Indicator seldom gives false whipsaw signals when the market is in a Trend Mode.

Chapter 10

THE INSTANTANEOUS
TRENDLINE

Never mistake motion for action.

—Ernest Hemingway

Perhaps the term *instantaneous* is a bit presumptuous to apply to the concepts we discuss in this chapter. Nonetheless, the term is somewhat appropriate in that our technology enables us to compute a continuous trendline from which we can rapidly assess market action. As derived from the Drunkard's Walk problem in Chapter 1, our model says the market consists of a Trend Mode and a Cycle Mode. It is more accurate to describe the general market as a combination of these two modes. Furthermore, in Chapter 3 we prove that we can completely eliminate the dominant cycle component by taking a Simple Moving Average (SMA) over the period of the cycle. If we take a simple average over the period of the dominant cycle on a bar-by-bar basis—because we have been able to identify a continuously varying dominant cycle—we basically have a variable-length moving average. This moving average is important because the dominant cycle component is always notched out. It follows that if the composite analytic waveform consists of only a trend component and a cycle component, and if we remove the cycle component, the residual must be the trend. Of course, this is not precisely true, because there will always be components other than the dominant cycle present. However, this is a workable

107

solution for trading purposes because the secondary cycles usually have a small amplitude.

We employ a 4-bar Weighted Moving Average (WMA) in conjunction with the Instantaneous Trendline to give an indication of when the price crosses the Instantaneous Trendline. Having only a 1-bar lag, the 4-bar WMA is useful for this purpose. One way to recognize the onset of a trend is to count backward from the current bar to the first crossing of the WMA and the Instantaneous Trendline. If the count is greater than a half-dominant cycle, you know that the market is in a Trend Mode. The reason for this is that if the market were in a Cycle Mode, we would expect the price to cross the Instantaneous Trendline every half cycle. Failure to do this is a clear indication of a Trend Mode. In fact, an amended rule might say that the onset of a Trend Mode is declared if the price has crossed more than a quarter cycle ago and does not appear to even try to head back across the Instantaneous Trendline. This amended rule will get you into a Trend Mode trade much earlier. However, as with all anticipatory signals, you will get caught in an error once in a while. A Trend Mode is over when the Smoothed Price crosses the Instantaneous Trendline.

Because we are taking an SMA over the entire period of the dominant cycle, the lag of an Instantaneous Trendline is one-half the dominant cycle. This lag is unavoidable. It is also possible to take an SMA over half the period of the dominant cycle. The half-period average has a quarter-cycle lag. The result is that the quarter-cycle average will cross the Instantaneous Trendline just as the Sinewave Indicator reaches a peak or valley. The half-period average crossing the Instantaneous Trendline can be used as a confirmation signal, which is another way of identifying when the price has reached a cyclic turning point.

The EasyLanguage code to compute the Instantaneous Trendline is given in Figure 10.1. As in computations in previous chapters, the code starts with the Hilbert Transform and measures the dominant cycle using the Homodyne Discriminator algorithm. The Instantaneous Trendline is computed by averaging the price over the integer number of bars of the smoothed dominant cycle. This average is smoothed in a 4-bar

```
Inputs:     Price((H+L)/2);

Vars: Smooth(0),
      Detrender(0),
      I1(0),
      Q1(0),
      jI(0),
      jQ(0),
      I2(0),
      Q2(0),
      Re(0),
      Im(0),
      Period(0),
      SmoothPeriod(0),
      SmoothPrice(0),
      DCPeriod(0),
      RealPart(0),
      ImagPart(0),
      count(0),
      ITrend(0),
      Trendline(0);

If CurrentBar > 5 then begin
      Smooth = (4*Price + 3*Price[1] + 2*Price[2] +
        Price[3]) / 10;
      Detrender = (.0962*Smooth + .5769*Smooth[2] -
        .5769*Smooth[4] - .0962*Smooth[6])*(.075*
        Period[1] + .54);

      {Compute InPhase and Quadrature components}
      Q1 = (.0962*Detrender + .5769*Detrender[2] -
        .5769*Detrender[4] - .0962*Detrender[6])*(.075*
        Period[1] + .54);
      I1 = Detrender[3];

      {Advance the phase of I1 and Q1 by 90 degrees}
      jI = (.0962*I1 + .5769*I1[2] - .5769*I1[4] -
        .0962*I1[6])*(.075*Period[1] + .54);
      jQ = (.0962*Q1 + .5769*Q1[2] - .5769*Q1[4] -
        .0962*Q1[6])*(.075*Period[1] + .54);

      {Phasor addition for 3 bar averaging)}
      I2 = I1 - jQ;
      Q2 = Q1 + jI;
                                        (continued)
```

Figure 10.1. EasyLanguage code to compute the Instantaneous Trendline.

```
{Smooth the I and Q components before applying
  the discriminator}
I2 = .2*I2 + .8*I2[1];
Q2 = .2*Q2 + .8*Q2[1];

{Homodyne Discriminator}
Re = I2*I2[1] + Q2*Q2[1];
Im = I2*Q2[1] - Q2*I2[1];
Re = .2*Re + .8*Re[1];
Im = .2*Im + .8*Im[1];
If Im <> 0 and Re <> 0 then Period =
  360/ArcTangent(Im/Re);
If Period > 1.5*Period[1] then Period =
  1.5*Period[1];
If Period < .67*Period[1] then Period =
  .67*Period[1];
If Period < 6 then Period = 6;
If Period > 50 then Period = 50;
Period = .2*Period + .8*Period[1];
SmoothPeriod = .33*Period + .67*SmoothPeriod[1];

{Compute Trendline as simple average over the
  measured dominant cycle period}
DCPeriod = IntPortion(SmoothPeriod + .5);
ITrend = 0;
For count = 0 to DCPeriod - 1 begin
    ITrend = ITrend + Price[count];
end;
If DCPeriod > 0 then ITrend = ITrend / DCPeriod;
Trendline = (4*ITrend + 3*ITrend[1] +
  2*ITrend[2] + ITrend[3]) / 10;
If CurrentBar < 12 then Trendline = Price;

SmoothPrice = (4*Price + 3*Price[1] +
  2*Price[2] + Price[3]) / 10;

Plot1(Trendline, "Trendline");
Plot2(SmoothPrice, "SP");

End;
```

Figure 10.1. *(Continued).*

WMA to make the Instantaneous Trendline a little smoother. The price itself is also smoothed in a 4-bar WMA to provide the second line of this indicator.

The actions of the Instantaneous Trendline and the Smoothed Price curves are shown in Figure 10.2. The Smoothed Price crosses the Instantaneous Trendline during the third week in August. The measured dominant cycle period during this time was about 22 bars (see Figure 7.7). Since the price does not even try to come back to the Instantaneous Trendline, we declare the trend in force about five days after the crossing, around the first of September. According to this indicator, the trend stays in force until the Smoothed Price crosses the Instantaneous Trendline again, in mid-January. Other indications from the Sinewave Indicator would have declared the trend over near the first of December, however. With reference to Figure 9.5, the Sinewave Indicator line crossing early in December signals a Cycle Mode buy signal.

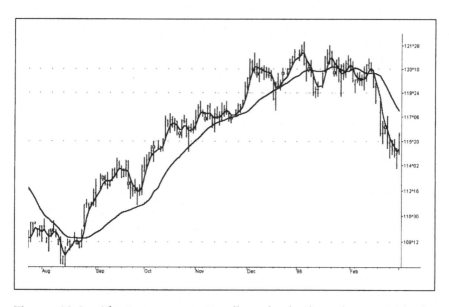

Figure 10.2. The Instantaneous Trendline clearly shows how to trade the trend.

Chart created with TradeStation 2000i® by Omega Research, Inc.

Key Points to Remember

- The Instantaneous Trendline is generated by removing the dominant cycle component of the composite waveform. This is done taking a simple average over the period of the dominant cycle.
- A trend is declared in force if the SmoothPrice has not crossed the Instantaneous Trendline within the previous half-dominant cycle.
- As a faster indication of the trend onset, a trend is declared if the Smoothed Price has not crossed the Instantaneous Trendline within the previous quarter-dominant cycle and does not appear to start in the crossing direction.
- A trend is over when the SmoothPrice crosses the Instantaneous Trendline.

Chapter 11

IDENTIFYING MARKET MODES

Invention is the mother of necessity.

—THORSTEIN VEBLEN

The simplified model of the market, derived from the Drunkard's Walk problem, has only two modes—the Cycle Mode and the Trend Mode. Through the derivation of the Sinewave Indicator and the Instantaneous Trendline, we have shown several ways to estimate which mode the market may have for a given moment. As with most technical indicators, the decision point between modes is not clear-cut. In fact, trying to automate the decision often leads to a great deal of chatter and rapid back and forth switching of decisions.

Since the Cycle Mode exists for the smallest fraction of time and since most traders make the most money following a trend rather than a cycle, it is best to assume that the market is in a Trend Mode unless some very specific criteria are met. There are only two criteria to establish a Cycle Mode. First, a Cycle Mode exists for the period of a half-dominant cycle after the crossing of the two Sinewave Indicator lines. Second, a Cycle Mode exists if the measured phase rate of change is more than two-thirds the phase rate of change of the dominant cycle (360/Period) and is less than 1.5 times the phase rate of change of the dominant cycle.

There is another condition that defines a Trend Mode. This condition is derived from pragmatic observation, not theoretical considerations. When the market makes a major reversal, it often does this with great vigor. When this occurs, the prices have a wide separation from the Instantaneous Trendline. When the prices are widely separated from the Instantaneous Trendline, it is possible for the Cycle Mode conditions to be met—but the Cycle Mode identification is clearly incorrect. I have therefore inserted another overriding rule for these cases. That rule is that if the SmoothPrice (the 4-bar WMA of the Price) is separated by more than 1.5 percent from the Instantaneous Trendline, then the correct market mode is the Trend Mode.

We can apply the mode identification in a TradeStation or SuperCharts Paintbar to visually identify the current market mode. In addition, the mode identification can be used as a code fragment as part of an automatic trading system to establish which set of trading rules will be employed. The EasyLanguage code to compute the market mode and identify it as a paintbar is given in Figure 11.1.

```
Inputs:     Price((H+L)/2);

Vars: Smooth(0),
      Detrender(0),
      I1(0),
      Q1(0),
      jI(0),
      jQ(0),
      I2(0),
      Q2(0),
      Re(0),
      Im(0),
      Period(0),
      SmoothPeriod(0),
      SmoothPrice(0),
      DCPeriod(0),
      RealPart(0),
      ImagPart(0),
      count(0),
      DCPhase(0),
                                        (continued)
```

Figure 11.1.   EasyLanguage code to identify the market mode.

```
        Itrend(0),
        Trendline(0),
        Trend(0),
        DaysInTrend(0);

If CurrentBar > 5 then begin
        Smooth = (4*Price + 3*Price[1] + 2*Price[2] +
          Price[3])/10;
        Detrender = (.0962*Smooth + .5769*Smooth[2] -
          .5769*Smooth[4] - .0962*Smooth[6])*(.075*
          Period[1] + .54);

        {Compute InPhase and Quadrature components}
        Q1 = (.0962*Detrender + .5769*Detrender[2] -
          .5769*Detrender[4] - .0962*Detrender[6])*(.075*
          Period[1] + .54);
        I1 = Detrender[3];

        {Advance the phase of I1 and Q1 by 90 degrees}
        jI = (.0962*I1 + .5769*I1[2] - .5769*I1[4] -
          .0962*I1[6])*(.075*Period[1] + .54);
        jQ = (.0962*Q1 + .5769*Q1[2] - .5769*Q1[4] -
          .0962*Q1[6])*(.075*Period[1] + .54);

        {Phasor addition for 3 bar averaging)}
        I2 = I1 - jQ;
        Q2 = Q1 + jI;

        {Smooth the I and Q components before applying
          the discriminator}
        I2 = .2*I2 + .8*I2[1];
        Q2 = .2*Q2 + .8*Q2[1];

        {Homodyne Discriminator}
        Re = I2*I2[1] + Q2*Q2[1];
        Im = I2*Q2[1] - Q2*I2[1];
        Re = .2*Re + .8*Re[1];
        Im = .2*Im + .8*Im[1];
        If Im <> 0 and Re <> 0 then Period =
          360/ArcTangent(Im/Re);
```

(continued)

Figure 11.1. *(Continued).*

```
If Period > 1.5*Period[1] then Period =
  1.5*Period[1];
If Period < .67*Period[1] then Period =
  .67*Period[1];
If Period < 6 then Period = 6;
If Period > 50 then Period = 50;
Period = .2*Period + .8*Period[1];
SmoothPeriod = .33*Period + .67*SmoothPeriod[1];

{Compute Dominant Cycle Phase}
SmoothPrice = (4*Price + 3*Price[1] + 2*
  Price[2] + Price[3])/10;
DCPeriod = IntPortion(SmoothPeriod + .5);
RealPart = 0;
ImagPart = 0;
For count = 0 To DCPeriod - 1 begin
        RealPart = RealPart + Cosine(360 * count
          / DCPeriod)*(SmoothPrice[count]);
        ImagPart = ImagPart + Sine(360 *
          count/DCPeriod)*(SmoothPrice[count]);

End;
If AbsValue(RealPart) >0 then DCPhase =
  Arctangent(ImagPart / RealPart);
If AbsValue(RealPart) <= 0.001 then DCPhase = 90*
  Sign(ImagPart);
DCPhase = DCPhase + 90;

{Compensate for one bar lag of the Weighted
  Moving Average}
DCPhase = DCPhase + 360 / SmoothPeriod;

If ImagPart < 0 then DCPhase = DCPhase + 180;
If DCPhase > 315 then DCPhase = DCPhase - 360;

{Compute Trendline as simple average over the
  measured dominant cycle period}
ITrend = 0;
For count = 0 to DCPeriod - 1 begin
        ITrend = ITrend + Price[count];
End;
```

                                                       (continued)

Figure 11.1.   *(Continued).*

```
If DCPeriod > 0 then ITrend = ITrend / DCPeriod;
Trendline = (4*ITrend + 3*ITrend[1] +
  2*ITrend[2] + ITrend[3])/10;
If CurrentBar < 12 then Trendline = Price;

{Assume Trend Mode}
Trend = 1;

{Measure days in trend from last crossing of the
  Sinewave Indicator lines}
If Sine(DCPhase) Crosses Over Sine(DCPhase + 45)
  or Sine(DCPhase) Crosses Under Sine(DCPhase +
  45) Then begin
        DaysInTrend = 0;
        Trend = 0;
End;
DaysInTrend = DaysInTrend + 1;
If DaysInTrend < .5*SmoothPeriod then Trend = 0;

{Cycle Mode if delta phase is +/- 50% of dominant
  cycle change of phase}
If SmoothPeriod <> 0 and (DCPhase - DCPhase[1] >
  .67*360/SmoothPeriod and DCPhase - DCPhase[1] <
  1.5*360/SmoothPeriod) then Trend = 0;

{Trend Mode if prices are widely separated from
  the Trendline}
If AbsValue((SmoothPrice - Trendline)/Trendline) >=
  .015 then Trend = 1;

{Paint Bar if in the Cycle Mode}
If Trend = 0 then begin
        Plot1(high, "high");
        Plot2(low, "low");
End;

End;
```

Figure 11.1. *(Continued).*

Key Points to Remember

- Assume the market is in a Trend Mode unless specific criteria are met.
- A Cycle Mode exists for a half-dominant cycle after the crossing of the Sinewave Indicator lines or when the measured phase rate of change is within ±50 percent of the phase rate of change of the dominant cycle.
- A Trend Mode is declared if the 4-bar WMA is separated from the Instantaneous Trendline by more than 1.5 percent.
- The market mode can be identified as a paintbar or used as a code fragment in an automatic trading system.

Chapter 12

DESIGNING A PROFITABLE TRADING SYSTEM

Truth and science triumph again over ignorance and superstition.

—JOHN EHLERS

In this chapter we develop a completely automatic trading system called the SineTrend Automatic System based on the rules that we develop in the previous chapters. Our fundamental approach is to trade using the Trend Mode rules when the market is in a Trend Mode and trade using the Cycle Mode rules when the market is in a Cycle Mode. The code shown in Figure 12.1 is a complete trading system using these rules strictly from a theoretical perspective. There is absolutely no accommodation for real trading situations or specific personalities of the commodity or stock being traded.

This code was first applied to the Treasury Bonds futures contract because the system trades both long and short with equal facility. The Treasury Bond data were a back-adjusted continuous contract covering the period from 9 July 1984 to 16 June 2000, a period of 15.54 years. (A back-adjusted continuous contract is created by stringing real contracts together and adjusting all prices in the previous contract by the price difference between contracts at the rollover date. The process is repeated for each new previous contract.) Adding a $1,000 money-management stop, the results right out of the box are shown in

```
Inputs:     Price((H+L)/2);

Vars: Smooth(0),
      Detrender(0),
      I1(0),
      Q1(0),
      jI(0),
      jQ(0),
      I2(0),
      Q2(0),
      Re(0),
      Im(0),
      Period(0),
      SmoothPeriod(0),
      SmoothPrice(0),
      DCPeriod(0),
      RealPart(0),
      ImagPart(0),
      count(0),
      DCPhase(0),
      DCSine(0),
      LeadSine(0),
      Itrend(0),
      Trendline(0),
      Trend(0),
      DaysInTrend(0);

If CurrentBar > 5 then begin
      Smooth = (4*Price + 3*Price[1] + 2*Price[2] +
        Price[3]) / 10;
      Detrender = (.0962*Smooth + .5769*Smooth[2] -
        .5769*Smooth[4] - .0962*Smooth[6])*(.075*
        Period[1] + .54);

      {Compute InPhase and Quadrature components}
      Q1 = (.0962*Detrender + .5769*Detrender[2] -
        .5769*Detrender[4] - .0962*Detrender[6])*
        (.075*Period[1] + .54);
      I1 = Detrender[3];
                                              (continued)
```

Figure 12.1.   EasyLanguage code for an Automatic SineTrend Trading System.

```
{Advance the phase of I1 and Q1 by 90 degrees}
jI = (.0962*I1 + .5769*I1[2] - .5769*I1[4] -
   .0962*I1[6])*(.075*Period[1] + .54);
jQ = (.0962*Q1 + .5769*Q1[2] - .5769*Q1[4] -
   .0962*Q1[6])*(.075*Period[1] + .54);

{Phasor addition for 3 bar averaging)}
I2 = I1 - jQ;
Q2 = Q1 + jI;

{Smooth the I and Q components before applying
   the discriminator}
I2 = .2*I2 + .8*I2[1].;
Q2 = .2*Q2 + .8*Q2[1];

{Homodyne Discriminator}
Re = I2*I2[1] + Q2*Q2[1];
Im = I2*Q2[1] - Q2*I2[1];
Re = .2*Re + .8*Re[1];
Im = .2*Im + .8*Im[1];
If Im <> 0 and Re <> 0 then Period =
   360/ArcTangent(Im/Re);
If Period > 1.5*Period[1] then Period =
   1.5*Period[1];
If Period < .67*Period[1] then Period =
   .67*Period[1];
If Period < 6 then Period = 6;
If Period > 50 then Period = 50;
Period = .2*Period + .8*Period[1];
SmoothPeriod = .33*Period + .67*SmoothPeriod[1];

{Compute Dominant Cycle Phase}
SmoothPrice = (4*Price + 3*Price[1] + 2*Price[2] +
   Price[3]) / 10;
DCPeriod = IntPortion(SmoothPeriod + .5);
RealPart = 0;
ImagPart = 0;
For count = 0 To DCPeriod - 1 begin
     RealPart = RealPart + Cosine(360 * count /
        DCPeriod) * (SmoothPrice[count]);
                                   (continued)
```

Figure 12.1.   *(Continued)*.

```
                  ImagPart = ImagPart + Sine(360 * count /
                  DCPeriod) * (SmoothPrice[count]);
End;
If AbsValue(RealPart) >0 then DCPhase =
  Arctangent(ImagPart / RealPart);
If AbsValue(RealPart) <= 0.001 then DCPhase =
  90 * Sign(ImagPart);
DCPhase = DCPhase + 90;

{Compensate for one bar lag of the Weighted
  Moving Average}
DCPhase = DCPhase + 360 / SmoothPeriod;

If ImagPart < 0 then DCPhase = DCPhase + 180;
If DCPhase > 315 then DCPhase = DCPhase - 360;

{Compute the Sine and LeadSine Indicators}
DCSine = Sine(DCPhase);
LeadSine = Sine(DCPhase + 45);

{Compute Trendline as simple average over the
  measured dominant cycle period}
ITrend = 0;
For count = 0 to DCPeriod - 1 begin
      ITrend = ITrend + Price[count];
End;
If DCPeriod > 0 then ITrend = ITrend / DCPeriod;
Trendline = (4*ITrend + 3*ITrend[1] + 2*ITrend[2] +
  ITrend[3]) / 10;
If CurrentBar < 12 then Trendline = Price;

{Assume Trend Mode}
Trend = 1;

{Measure days in trend from last crossing of the
  Sinewave Indicator lines}
If Sine(DCPhase) Crosses Over Sine(DCPhase + 45)
  or Sine(DCPhase) Crosses Under Sine(DCPhase +
  45) Then begin
      DaysInTrend = 0;
      Trend = 0;
End;
```

                                                    (continued)

Figure 12.1.   *(Continued).*

```
      DaysInTrend = DaysInTrend + 1;
      If DaysInTrend < .5*SmoothPeriod then Trend = 0;

      {Cycle Mode if delta phase is +/- 50% of dominant
        cycle change of phase}
      If SmoothPeriod <> 0 and (DCPhase - DCPhase[1] >
        .67*360/SmoothPeriod and DCPhase - DCPhase[1] <
        1.5*360/SmoothPeriod) then Trend = 0;

      {Declare a Trend Mode if the SmoothPrice is more
        than 1.5% from the Trendline}
      If AbsValue((SmoothPrice - Trendline)/Trendline) >=
        .015 then Trend = 1;

      If Trend = 1 then begin
            If Trend[1] = 0 then begin
                  If MarketPosition = -1 and Smooth
                      Price >= Trendline then buy;
                  If MarketPosition = 1 and SmoothPrice <
                      Trendline then sell;
            End;
            If SmoothPrice Crosses Over Trendline
              then buy;
            If SmoothPrice Crosses Under Trendline
              then sell;
      End;

      If Trend = 0 then begin
            If LeadSine Crosses Over DCSine then buy;
            If LeadSine Crosses Under DCSine then
              sell;
      End;

End;
```

Figure 12.1. *(Continued).*

Figure 12.2. Phenomenal! The $398 average profit per trade with a 40 percent success rate on only $12,500 maximum drawdown is competitive with any commercially available Treasury Bond trading system. About 80 percent of the profits were made on long side trades.

I was curious as to how much of the action was contributed by the Trend Mode and how much was contributed by the Cycle Mode. I therefore simply deleted the four lines of code that made the Cycle Mode trades and ran the system again on the same Treasury Bond data. The results of the Trend Mode–only trading are given in Figure 12.3.

These results are simply awful! The average profit per trade dropped to negative territory before any rational allowance for

Total Net Profit	$92,875.00		
Gross Profit	$201,031.25	Gross Loss	($108,156.25)
Total # of trades	233	Percent profitable	40.77%
Number winning trades	95	Number losing trades	138
Largest winning trade	$15,468.75	Largest losing trade	($1,156.25)
Average winning trade	$2,116.12	Average losing trade	($783.74)
Ratio avg win/ avg loss	2.70	Avg trade (win & loss)	$398.61
Max consec. Winners	5	Max consec. losers	11
Avg # bars in winners	20	Avg # bars in losers	5
Max intraday drawdown	($12,500.00)		
Profit Factor	1.86	Max # contracts held	1

Figure 12.2. Original SineTrend performance summary on Treasury Bonds— 9 July 1984 to 16 June 2000.

Total Net Profit	$19,968.75		
Gross Profit	$39,093.75	Gross Loss	($59,062.50)
Total # of trades	81	Percent profitable	18.52%
Number winning trades	15	Number losing trades	66
Largest winning trade	$8,218.75	Largest losing trade	($1,000.00)
Average winning trade	$2,606.25	Average losing trade	($894.89)
Ratio avg win/ avg loss	2.91	Avg trade (win & loss)	$246.53
Max consec. Winners	2	Max consec. losers	12
Avg # bars in winners	38	Avg # bars in losers	8
Max intraday drawdown	($23,343.75)		
Profit Factor	0.66	Max # contracts held	1

Figure 12.3. SineTrend trend only performance summary on Treasury Bonds—9 July 1984 to 16 June 2000.

slippage and commission! The first thing these results indicate is that the system is being carried by Cycle Mode trades. At this point, it seems prudent to make a concession to real-world realities and try to modify the Trend Mode rules. One of the easiest things to do is change the computation of the Instantaneous Trendline. By increasing or decreasing the Instantaneous Trendline SMA length, the resulting Instantaneous Trendline will be either more reactive or will react slower. If we change the code by using a CycPart multiplier, the SMA length is still related to the period of the measured dominant cycle. The code fragment for the Trendline calculation was changed as indicated in Figure 12.4. After changing the code, optimizing on a CycPart of 1.15, and increasing the money-management stop to $1,100, the results indicated in Figure 12.5 were obtained. These changes and optimizations are not "curve fitting" because the testing

```
{Compute Trendline as simple average over the
  measured dominant cycle period}
ITrend = 0;
IntPeriod = IntPortion(CycPart*SmoothPeriod + .5);
For count = 0 to IntPeriod - 1 begin
     ITrend = ITrend + Price[count];
End;
If DCPeriod > 0 then ITrend = ITrend / IntPeriod;
Trendline = (4*ITrend + 3*ITrend[1] + 2*ITrend[2] +
  ITrend[3]) / 10;
If CurrentBar < 12 then Trendline = Price;
```

Figure 12.4. Code fragment for optimizable Instantaneous Trendline calculation.

Total Net Profit	$113,525.00		
Gross Profit	$205,000.00	Gross Loss	($91,475.00)
Total # of trades	191	Percent profitable	44.5%
Number winning trades	85	Number losing trades	106
Largest winning trade	$16,062.50	Largest losing trade	($1,125.00)
Average winning trade	$2,411.76	Average losing trade	($862.97)
Ratio avg win/ avg loss	2.79	Avg trade (win & loss)	$594.37
Max consec. winners	5	Max consec. losers	8
Avg # bars in winners	24	Avg # bars in losers	6
Max intraday drawdown	($8,137.50)		
Profit Factor	2.24	Max # contracts held	1

Figure 12.5. SineTrend performance summary on Treasury Bonds, modified CycPart = 1.15, money-management stop = $1,100—9 July 1984 to 16 June 2000.

covered a 16-year span and the results carry a substantial trade-to-parameter ratio.

These results are outstanding! The net profit has been increased by 22 percent over the original system. The increased net profit and reduced number of trades have produced nearly a 50 percent increase in the average profit per trade. Further, the maximum drawdown over the 15-year period was reduced by 35 percent. Incidentally, going back and checking on the Trend Mode-only performance after the Instantaneous Trendline was optimized, I got the results shown in Figure 12.6. Now the Trend Mode has been enhanced to carry its share of the load. The optimization resulted from a minor increase in the period to calculate the Instantaneous Trendline.

Total Net Profit	$43,062.50		
Gross Profit	$98,906.00	Gross Loss	($55,843.75)
Total # of trades	67	Percent profitable	35.82%
Number winning	24	Number losing trades	43
Largest winning trade	$16,062.50	Largest losing trade	($1,781.25)
Average winning trade	$4,121.09	Average losing trade	($1,298.69)
Ratio avg win/ avg loss	3.17	Avg trade (win & loss)	$642.72
Max consec. Winners	4	Max consec. losers	6
Avg # bars in winners	52	Avg # bars in losers	13
Max intraday drawdown	($10,956.25)		
Profit Factor	1.77	Max # contracts held	1

Figure 12.6. SineTrend performance summary on Treasury Bonds (Trend Mode–only), modified CycPart = 1.15, money-management stop = $1,500— 9 July 1984 to 16 June 2000.

The continuous and sustained equity growth of this Sine-Trend Automatic System over the 15-year period indicates just how robust this system is. A major contribution to its robustness is the fact that the underlying principles of the system were based purely on theoretical considerations. Equity growth is shown in Figure 12.7.

The obvious question to ask now is whether the SineTrend Automatic System works with contracts other than Treasury Bonds. Since the system is based purely on theory, the answer is that it should be universal. There are bound to be some issues for which it trades better than others, however. To test the premise that it can be applied to other securities, I applied the modified SineTrend to the back-adjusted Swiss Franc futures contract over the period from 13 February 1975 to 1 June 2000. When the Cyc-Part input was optimized for 1.10 and the money-management stop was set at $2,200, I obtained the results shown in Figure 12.8.

The results of the SineTrend Automatic Trading System are more than respectable—they are on par with the results obtained by most commercially available trading systems. The average

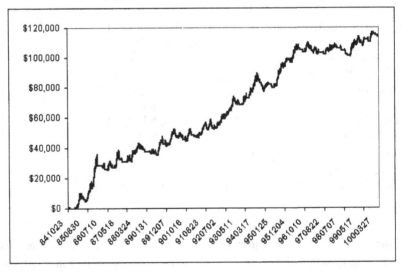

Figure 12.7. Equity Curve.

Total Net Profit	$139,212.50		
Gross Profit	$366,575.00	Gross Loss	($227,362.50)
Total # of trades	460	Percent profitable	50.87%
Number winning trades	234	Number losing trades	226
Largest winning trade	$12,712.50	Largest losing trade	($3,200.00)
Average winning trade	$1,566.56	Average losing trade	($1,006.03)
Ratio avg win/ avg loss	1.56	Avg trade (win & loss)	$302.64
Max consec. winners	9	Max consec. losers	8
Avg # bars in winners	16	Avg # bars in losers	7
Max intraday drawdown	($18,187.50)		
Profit Factor	1.61	Max # contracts held	1

Figure 12.8. SineTrend performance summary on Deutschemark, modified Cyc-Part = 1.10, money-management stop = $2,200—13 February 1975 to 1 June 2000.

profit per trade is $302. The probability of success is over 50 percent. The ratio of average win to average loss is 1.56:1. Joe Krutsinger calls this the "daddy-goes-to-town number," meaning that every time daddy goes to town he brings home $1.50 when he is a winner as opposed to giving up $1 when he is a loser.

The SineTrend system, as presented, is just a core from which much more sophisticated and profitable systems can be spawned. The trading rules I have provided are extremely simple. There is an infinite number of ways these rules can be enhanced. For example, we know the Sinewave Indicator crosses one-eighth of a cycle before the turning point. For longer cycle periods, we could be entering and exiting the Cycle Mode trades too early. It would not be terribly difficult to add a lag factor relating to the measured period before entering Cycle Mode trades. There may even be better or more reactive ways to switch between the Trend Mode and the Cycle Mode. A correct mode determination is bound to have a profound effect on the trading system because deciding the mode is the primary decision to be made before the rules are applied. It is my desire to turn you loose on making the system better. I look forward to hearing of your successes.

Key Points to Remember

- The SineTrend Automatic Trading System switches trading rules depending on the mode of the market.
- In the Trend Mode, trades are made on the basis of the SmoothPrice crossing the Instantaneous Trendline.
- In the Cycle Mode, trades are made on the basis of the crossing of the Sinewave Indicator lines.
- The automatic trading system based on theoretical principles performs on par with commercially available systems right out of the box.

Chapter 13

TRANSFORM ARITHMETIC

*The real danger is not that computers will begin to
think like men, but that men will
begin to think like computers.*

—Sydney J. Harris

The purpose for invoking transform arithmetic is to apply a tool
toward solving a differential equation problem by using simple
algebra. Without this tool, many of the problems we encounter
would be intractable. There are many kinds of transforms. For
example, Mellin and Legendre Transforms exist for working in
cylindrical and spherical coordinates. Hankel and Meijer Transforms exist for working with Bessel Functions. The list goes on
and on.

The data with which we deal in trading are sampled data. We
get a sample of the data once per bar regardless of the time frame
of the sample. Many price charts are displayed as daily data. The
sampling basis is equally valid for other sampling periods, such
as weekly, hourly, or even one-minute bars. All information
scales to the sampling period. The correct transform tool to use
for this data is the Z Transform. We describe the Z Transform in
this chapter so that we can later assess the transfer characteristics of more complicated filters. It is instructive to review
several other transforms so that we can relate our problem solutions to real-world situations, achieving greater insight into
both the problem and its solution. Because most traders have
had no previous exposure to this powerful tool, I explain transform arithmetic in the simplest possible manner and only in
terms of how it applies to trading.

Laplace Transform

The Laplace Transform is used, among other purposes, to solve for the transient conditions in electrical circuits. As an illustration, a simple electrical circuit is shown in Figure 13.1. A transient occurs after the switch is closed. We will show the solution for how the voltage V changes as a function of time after the switch is closed. From physics we know that the current flowing through a capacitor is proportional to the size of the capacitor and the rate change of voltage across it. The equation for current flow is

$$I = C\,\frac{dV}{dt}$$

After the switch is closed, current flows through the resistor, through the capacitor, and is returned to the battery that has a voltage E. From *Ohm's Law*, the voltage V is the battery voltage less the current multiplied by the Resistance R. That is,

$$V = E - IR = E - RC\,\frac{dV}{dt}$$

We now have a differential equation to solve for V as a function of time. Differential equations are pretty scary stuff, so let us

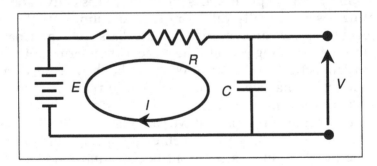

Figure 13.1.   A simple electrical circuit for transient analysis.

invoke the Laplace Transform by substituting the Laplace Operator S for the calculus operator (d/dt). Our equation now becomes

$$V = E - RCSV$$

$$\frac{V}{RC} = \frac{E}{RC} - SV$$

$$V\left(S + \frac{1}{RC}\right) = \frac{E}{RC}$$

$$V = \frac{\frac{1}{RC}}{S + \frac{1}{RC}} E$$

Amazing! We have solved the problem for the voltage V using only simple algebra. More precise, V is a function of the Laplace Operator, and should be written as

$$V(s) = \frac{\frac{1}{RC}}{S + \frac{1}{RC}} E$$

In general, the output function $Y(s)$ is equal to the input function $X(s)$ multiplied by the system *transfer response* $H(s)$. In other words, the system transfer response is the $X(s)/Y(s)$ ratio.

We really want the solution for voltage as a function of time. The way we do this is to compare the relationship between the Laplace Transform and the solution in the time domain. Transform pairs for these solutions can be found in many handbooks and textbooks on the subject. In this case, we find that the transform pair is

$$\frac{a}{S + a} \Rightarrow \left(1 - e^{-at}\right)$$

By examining like terms, we immediately have the solution for voltage in the time domain as

$$V(t) = E(1 - e^{-t/RC})$$

Thus, we have solved a relatively complex differential equation using the Laplace Transform and simple algebra. In the S Domain, the output is the input multiplied by the transfer response of the system. In other words, the transfer response is the ratio of the input to the output. In this format, the transfer function can describe filters independent of the input driving function. In our example, the input is the constant battery voltage E. This input is multiplied in the S Domain (and in the time domain because it is a constant) by the transfer response of the RC filter. We will see this form of equation again when we examine Z Transforms.

Fourier Transform

What Laplace Transforms are for transient analysis, Fourier Transforms are for steady-state analysis. Recalling that the expression for complex frequency is $e^{j\omega t}$, when we take the derivative of the complex frequency we get $d(e^{j\omega t})/dt = j\omega\, e^{j\omega t}$. So the Fourier Transform operator for the rate of change is $j\omega$ instead of S. The Fourier and Laplace Transforms share many common characteristics.

Fourier Transforms are the tools we use to describe relationships in the time domain and frequency domain. For example, an impulse in the frequency domain is a definition of a pure monotonic cycle. This cycle is a sine wave in the time domain. Fourier Transforms have many applications for the solution of physical problems. For example, the relationship between the pattern across a lens and the projected image constitute a Fourier Transform pair. Similarly, the relationship between the aperture distribution of an antenna and the radiation pattern, somewhat analogous to a flashlight beam, is a Fourier Transform pair.

Z Transform

Just as Laplace and Fourier Transforms are powerful tools for continuous systems, Z Transforms provide a corresponding powerful tool for discrete systems. There are significant parallels between Z Transforms and Fourier Transforms. The Z Transform can be multiplied by the transfer response of a system to obtain a Z Transform of the system output. The sampled data output for a discrete system can be found by taking the inverse Z Transform. Because this theory is so important to digital signal processing, a brief review of Z Transform theory is in order.

We begin by defining a sequence of samples of the form x_0, x_1, x_2, x_3, and so on. We designate the sequence of values by $\{x(nT)\}$, or because the sampling period T can be considered unity, simply $\{x(n)\}$. The sequence may consist of a finite number of samples or can be infinite in extent. The Z Transform of the sequence is given as

$$Z\{x(n)\} = \sum_{n=0}^{\infty} x(n)z^{-n}$$

since all values of x are 0 for $n < 0$. Suppose the sequence $\{x(n)\}$ consists of an infinity of values as

$$\{x(n)\} = \{a, a^2, a^3, a^4, \ldots\} = (a)^n$$

where $a < 0$. The Z Transform for the sequence is

$$X(z) = \sum_{n=0}^{\infty} x(n)z^{-n} = \sum_{n=0}^{\infty} (a)^n z^{-n} = \sum_{n=0}^{\infty} (az^{-1})^n$$

Designating the common ratio as $r = az^{-1}$, the Z Transform is recognized as the geometric progression $1, r, r^2, r^3, r^4, \ldots$. The sum of the terms of this progression is

$$S = \frac{1 - r^n}{1 - r}$$

Since r is less than unity and n approaches infinity, the sum simplifies to $S = 1/(1 - r)$. Substituting $r = az^{-1}$, we obtain

$$X(z) = \frac{1}{1 - az^{-1}} = \frac{z}{z - a}$$

We can now find the Z Transform of a step function where $x(n) = 0$ for $n < 0$ and $x(n) = 1$ for $n \geq 0$. In this case,

$$X(z) = \sum_{n=0}^{\infty} z^{-n} = \frac{z}{z - 1}$$

One of the more interesting and useful properties of the Z Transform is the effect of a one sample delay on a function. Suppose a sequence is given by

$$\{x(n)\} = \{X(0), X(1), X(2), \ldots\}$$

the Z Transform of this sequence is

$$X(z) = x(0) + x(1)z^{-1} + x(2)z^{-2} + x(3)z^{-3} + \ldots$$

Now, suppose the sequence is delayed by one sample time. The Z Transform of the output sequence then is given by

$$Y(z) = x(0)z^{-1} + x(1)z^{-2} + x(2)z^{-3} + \ldots$$

Or simply

$$Y(z) = X(z)z^{-1}$$

That is, a one sample time delay is equivalent to multiplying the Z Transform by z^{-1}. An additional delay results in an additional factor of z^{-1}, and so on. This can be seen in equation form as

$$x(n) \rightarrow x(z)$$
$$x(n - 1) \rightarrow x(z)z^{-1}$$
$$x(n - 2) \rightarrow x(z)z^{-2}$$
$$\vdots$$

For a transform to work, there must be an inversion. Since $Z\{x(n)\} = X(z)$, then the inverse operation is written as $Z^{-1}\{X(z)\} = x(n)$. There are several ways to obtain the inverse transform, but perhaps the easiest is suggested by the original definition of the Z Transform. The expansion of $X(z)$ into a sum of inverse powers of z will exhibit $x(n)$ as coefficients of the expansion. When $X(z)$ is a rational fraction, the expansion can be made by long division. For example, we can find the Inverse Z Transform for the step function whose Z Transform was

$$X(z) = \frac{z}{z-1}$$

Performing the long division, we obtain

$$
\begin{array}{r}
1 + z^{-1} + z^{-2} + z^{-3} + \ldots \\
z-1 \overline{)z} \\
z - 1 \\
1 \\
1 - z^{-1} \\
z^{-1} \\
z^{-1} - z^{-2} \\
z^{-2} \\
z^{-2} - z^{-3} \\
z^{-3}
\end{array}
$$

We have thus re-created the original step function with which we started. We can also create some common Z Transform pairs by inspection. For example, we know that

$$Z\{a^n\} = \frac{z}{z-a}$$

We can substitute $e^{-kT} = e^{-k}$ for a (since e^{-k} is a number less than unity and the sampling period is unity) and obtain

$$Z\{e^{-kn}\} = \frac{z}{z - e^{-k}}$$

We now have a transform pair for an exponential function.

Another obvious transform pair exists for an impulse function. The impulse function will have a value only during the first sample. Its Z Transform is therefore unity. It follows that the impulse delayed by q samples is z^{-q}.

Approximations of Analog Transfer Functions

Occasionally, it is desirable to convert a known analog transfer function in the S Domain into a digital transfer function. This is most often done with the transfer function of a low-pass or band-pass filter, such as a Butterworth or Chebyshev type, because of the wealth of development and experience with these filters. There are two ways to perform this conversion. We describe only the impulse invariant method because it directly relates the electrical circuit described earlier in this chapter to an Exponential Moving Average (EMA).

The impulse invariant method consists of finding the impulse response of the analog filter $h(t)$ and setting $t = nT$. The Z Transform of the quantized impulse response is taken so that $H(z) = Z\{h(nT)\}$. It is key to factor the analog transfer response and use a partial fraction expansion so that the equation can be written in the following form:

$$H(s) = \sum_{i=1}^{N} \frac{A_i}{(S - p_i)}$$

where p_i represents the ith pole (the point at which the denominator goes to zero), A_i is the magnitude associated with the ith pole, and N is the number of poles. The impulse response is given by the Inverse Laplace Transform, which has the following form:

$$h(t) = \sum_{i=1}^{N} A_i e^{p_i t}$$

Since each pole in the S Domain gives rise to an exponential term in the time domain, at the sample times we have

$$h(nT) = \sum_{i=1}^{N} A_i e^{p_i nt}$$

We have derived the Z Transform of an exponential as

$$Z\{e^{-nkT}\} = \frac{z}{z - e^{-kt}}$$

Therefore, the Z Transform of the impulse response is

$$H(z) = \sum_{i=1}^{N} \frac{A_i z}{(z - e^{p_i t})}$$

Recalling that the transfer response of the resistor-capacitor analog filter is given by

$$H(s) = \frac{\dfrac{1}{RC}}{S + \dfrac{1}{RC}}$$

The transfer response has a single pole located at $S = -1/RC$. We can immediately substitute like terms to obtain the digital transfer response to be

$$H(z) = \frac{\dfrac{z}{RC}}{z - e^{-T/RC}}$$

Simplifying, by letting $(1 - \alpha) = e^{-T/RC}$, the equation becomes

$$H(z) = \frac{Az}{z - (1 - \alpha)}$$

and the frequency response of the digital filter transfer response is given as

$$H(e^{j\omega T}) = \frac{Ae^{j\omega T}}{e^{j\omega T} - (1 - \alpha)}$$

The critical, or cutoff, frequency is that point at which the amplitude of the two terms in the denominator are equal. Since $\omega = 2\pi/P_o$, where P_o is the period corresponding to the cutoff frequency, the critical period is

$$e^{-2\pi/P_o} = (1 - \alpha)$$

$$\frac{-2\pi}{P_o} = \ln(1 - \alpha)$$

$$P_o = \frac{-2\pi}{\ln(1 - \alpha)}$$

This is exactly the cutoff period we asserted for an EMA in Chapter 3. Alternatively, if we know the desired cutoff period, we can calculate the EMA α as

$$\alpha = 1 - e^{-2\pi/P_o}$$

Let us look at the transfer response in greater depth.

$$H(z) = \frac{Az}{z - (1 - \alpha)}$$

$$= \frac{A}{1 - (1 - \alpha)z^{-1}}$$

$$\frac{Y(z)}{X(z)} = \frac{A}{1 - (1 - \alpha)z^{-1}}$$

$$Y(z) - (1 - \alpha)Y(z)z^{-1} = AX(z)$$

Converting to the digital domain, and noting that z^{-1} notates a one period delay, we get

$$y - (1 - \alpha)y[1] = Ax$$
$$y = Ax + (1 - \alpha)y[1]$$

If we have a step function input of unity amplitude, the output must also reach unity when the number of periods is large. Therefore, A must equal α. We conclude that the digital equivalent of our resistor-capacitor is

$$y = \alpha x + (1 - \alpha)y[1]$$

This is exactly the equation for an EMA. In other words, the EMA is the equivalent of a RC low-pass filter in the physical world.

Key Points to Remember

- Transform arithmetic is used to algebraically solve differential equation or difference equation problems that would be intractable otherwise.
- In the Z Domain, the output is equal to the product of the input and the transfer response.
- The transfer response describes the performance of filters independently from the input driving function.
- Laplace, Fourier, and Z Transforms are related.

Chapter 14

FINITE IMPULSE RESPONSE FILTERS

There is nothing permanent except change.

—HERACLITUS

A Simple Moving Average (SMA) is one example of a Finite Impulse Response (FIR) filter. Spoken, these filters are alternatively pronounced "eff-eye-are" or "fur" filters. FIR filters have no corollary in the physical world—they exist only as digital computations. Their unique characteristic is that their impulse response is exactly the same as their coefficients. An impulse as input digital data is simply unity for one sample and zero for all other samples. As this impulse ages out, that is, as it is successively delayed, it excites each element of the filter successively, sweeping out the amplitude of the filter coefficients. Thus, the impulse response is the same as the filter coefficients. The general time response of a FIR filter is

$$y_n = h_0 x + h_1 x[1] + h_2 x[2] + h_3 x[3] \ldots h_{(N-1)} x[N-1]$$

Or, more concisely

$$y_n = \sum_{i=0}^{N-1} h_i x[N-i]$$

Taking the Z Transform gives us

$$Y(z) = \sum_{i=0}^{N-1} h_i X(z) z^{-i}$$

so that the transfer response is

$$H(z) = \frac{Y(z)}{X(z)} = \sum_{i=0}^{N-1} h_i z^{-i}$$

Note that if the transfer response is expressed as a rational fraction, the response of the FIR filter is all zeros. That is, there is no denominator other than unity. From the fundamental theorem of algebra, the Nth order polynomial describing the transfer response can be factored into N terms, each of which is a zero of the polynomial. Moving average filters are characterized as having all-zero responses.

The lag of a FIR filter is equal to the location along the filter where the sum of the coefficients is equal to half the sum of coefficients in the entire filter. In mathematical form, this condition is expressed as

$$\sum_{i=1}^{Lag} h_i = \frac{1}{2} \sum_{i=1}^{N-1} h_i$$

Note that the first coefficient, the one with zero lag, is not used. Perhaps an easier way to picture the lag is to imagine the filter coefficients describing the height of a geometrical shape. If you were to draw this shape on a piece of paper and cut it out with a pair of scissors, the lag would be equal to the center of gravity. That is, it would be equal to the balance point of the shape. FIR filters are usually symmetric about their center so that lag is exactly the center of the filter.

Weighted Moving Averages (WMA) are FIR filters that are not symmetric about their center point. This gives them the advantage of having less lag. The output of a 4-bar WMA is

$$y = (4x + 3x[1] + 2x[2] + x[3])/10$$

so that the coefficients are 4, 3, 2, and 1. Discarding the first coefficient, we see that the second coefficient is equal to the sum of all the coefficients (excluding the first). Therefore, a 4-bar WMA has a 1-bar lag. As a second example, the output of a 7-bar WMA is

$$y = (7x + 6x[1] + 5x[2] + 4x[3] + 3x[4] + 2x[5] + x[6])/28$$

In this case, the coefficients are 7, 6, 5, 4, 3, 2, and 1. After discarding the first zero-lag coefficient, the sum of the next two coefficients is equal to half the total sum. Therefore, a 7-bar WMA has a lag of 2 bars.

A big advantage of symmetrical FIR filters is that lag is constant regardless of the frequency of the signal being applied to the input of the filter. This means that there is no time distortion due to the filtering. The phase lag will be linear. Suppose the time lag is 4 bars. This means there is 180 degrees of phase lag to an 8-bar cycle period, 90 degrees of phase lag to a 16-bar cycle period, and only 45 degrees of phase lag to a 32-bar cycle period.

The phase lag that results from a WMA is nearly linear throughout the passband of the filter. One nice thing about the WMA is that higher-frequency components at and above the critical band-pass frequency are delayed less than the frequency components within the passband. This means that distortion tends to work in favor of the trader by delaying the higher-frequency wiggles less than the lag of the smoothed output.

The truth is that many of the benefits of FIR filters are unavailable to traders because the length of the filter must be relatively long to synthesize interesting passbands. As a result, the induced lag is prohibitive. However, we can perform some innovative tricks and put FIR filters to good use. For example, in Chapter 3 we showed how an SMA length can be adjusted to notch out undesired frequency components. Figure 3.5 is repeated here as Figure 14.1 to demonstrate this effect. The SMA has a notch in its frequency response for those cycle components having an integer number of cycles across the width of the filter.

An SMA is a FIR filter that has uniform amplitude coefficients. The transfer response can be viewed as a rectangle over the finite duration of the filter. The Fourier Transform of this rectangle is a $Sin(X)/X$ distribution, which is exactly what is dis-

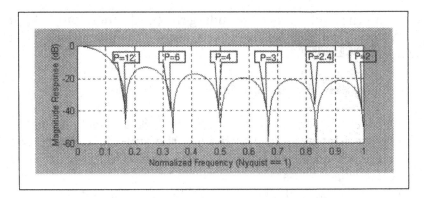

Figure 14.1.   Frequency response of a 12-bar SMA.

played in Figure 14.1. The numerator of this function goes to zero each time X goes through a multiple of 180 degrees. If L is the length of the FIR filter and P is the period of the signal variable being applied to it, the frequency response of the SMA FIR filter in radian measure is

$$H(\omega) = \frac{Sin\left(\dfrac{\pi L}{P}\right)}{\dfrac{\pi L}{P}}$$

Note that the $Sin(X)/X$ distribution has lobes in the response between the notches. Smoothing the time-domain response can lower these lobes. This means we must taper the coefficients of the FIR filter. When we taper the coefficients of the filter, the end elements have a smaller contribution to the filtering action than they do in the uniform amplitude case. The result is that there is less filtering action for a given length FIR-tapered filter when compared to the uniform amplitude coefficient case of the SMA. We therefore have a trade-off between the degree of out-of-band filtering and the efficiency of filtering the passband. A number of amplitude tapers have been invented, each with a desired characteristic for out-of-band signal rejection. It is im-

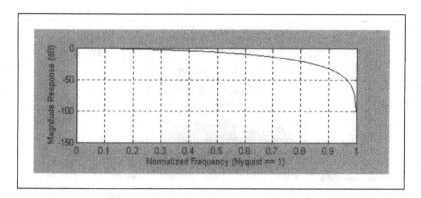

Figure 14.2. Amplitude response of a three-element linearly tapered FIR filter.

practical for traders to employ these tapers, however, because of the additional lag induced by passband inefficiency. Linear coefficient tapers are adequate for most trading applications.

It might be instructive to examine the passband of several linearly tapered FIR filters. Starting with one of the shortest possible, a three-element filter has a response of

$$y = (x + 2x[1] + x[2])/4$$

The lag through this filter is just to the center of the filter, which is 1 bar. Its amplitude response is shown in Figure 14.2. The normalized frequency corresponds to a 2-bar period. So this short filter is only useful for canceling the 2-bar cycle.

The next longest FIR-tapered filter has four elements. Its response is

$$Y = (x + 2x[1] + 2x[2] + x[3])/6$$

The lag through this filter is 1.5 bars to the center of the filter. Its amplitude response is shown in Figure 14.3. The additional term has introduced a second null for a 3-bar cycle at a normalized frequency of 0.67. (The way to navigate between the normalized frequency and the cycle period is to divide the normalized frequency by 2 and then invert.) The cutoff fre-

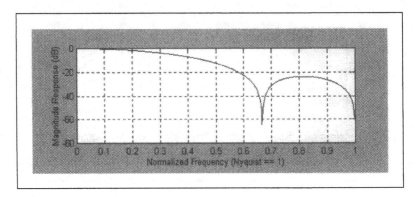

Figure 14.3.   Amplitude response of a four-element linearly tapered FIR filter.

quency, the point at which the amplitude response is –3 dB, is at a normalized frequency of about 0.33. This corresponds to a 6-bar cycle.

Continuing our sequence of successively longer tapered FIR filters, the response of a 5-bar filter is

$$Y = (x + 2x[1] + 3x[2] + 2x[4] + x[5])/9$$

The lag of this filter—the distance to its center—is 2 bars. The amplitude of this 5-bar tapered FIR filter is shown in Figure 14.4.

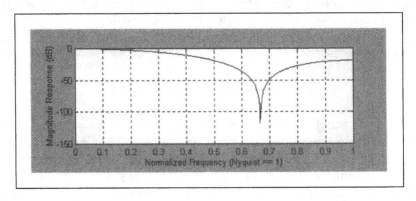

Figure 14.4.   Amplitude response of a five-element linearly tapered FIR filter.

We can see that something interesting has happened. The cancellation of the 2-bar cycle has been lost. Although it is difficult to see on the large amplitude scale, the cutoff frequency has been reduced when compared to that of the 4-bar filter, but not by much. This filter does not seem to be of much use.

By contrast, a six-element linearly tapered FIR filter has some very interesting characteristics. Its time-domain response is

$$Y = (x + 2x[1] + 3x[2] + 3x[3] + 2x[4] + x[5])/12$$

The lag through this filter is 2.5 bars to the center of the filter. Its amplitude response is shown in Figure 14.5. Not only has the cancellation of the 2-bar cycle period returned, but also the cutoff frequency has been reduced to about 0.2, a 10-bar cycle. Furthermore, the 3-bar and 4-bar cycles have been notched out by this filter. Attenuation between the notches is not uniform, but is nonetheless substantial. This is an excellent filter for general-purpose use by traders.

We can now continue with our filter sequence. In so doing, we would find that we would prefer to have an even number of elements in our tapered FIR filter so that the normalized unity frequency, a 2-bar cycle, is always notched out. Longer and longer cycles constitute the passband as the length of the filter is increased, with the cutoff period being about 1.5 times the length

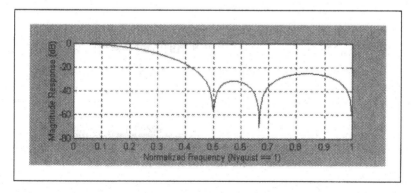

Figure 14.5.   Amplitude response of a six-element linearly tapered FIR filter.

of the filter. Never forget that the lag of an N-length filter is $(N-1)/2$. Lag is the most crucial parameter of filter performance for a trader.

Key Points to Remember

- A Simple Moving Average (SMA) is a Finite Impulse Response (FIR) filter with uniform amplitude filter coefficients.
- Symmetrical FIR filters have no time distortion and, therefore, have a linear phase delay.
- The lag of a FIR filter is the center of gravity of the filter coefficients.
- A Weighted Moving Average (WMA) has linear phase delay across its passband.
- A WMA always has less lag outside the passband than it has for cycle components within the passband.
- A 4-bar WMA has a lag of 1 bar.
- A 7-bar WMA has a lag of 2 bars.
- A six-element symmetrically, linearly tapered FIR filter is one of trading's most interesting and useful filters.
- The passband period of a symmetrically, linearly tapered FIR filter is approximately 1.5 times the length of the filter.

Chapter 15

INFINITE IMPULSE
RESPONSE FILTERS

Everyone is a child of his past.

—EDNA G. ROSTOW

An Exponential Moving Average (EMA) is one example of an Infinite Impulse Response (IIR) filter. Spoken, these filters are almost always pronounced "eye-eye-are" filters. As the name implies, IIR filters ring out forever (in theory) after being stimulated by an impulse excitation, just like a bell. These filters are the digital equivalent of filters that can, and have, been designed and constructed from physical world components. As we show in Chapter 13, an EMA is one example of an IIR filter. The transfer response of the EMA is shown to be

$$H(z) = \frac{\alpha}{1 - (1 - \alpha)z^{-1}}$$

As opposed to the all-zero response of the FIR filter, the transfer response of the IIR filter is expressed as a rational fraction. When we examine the Z Transform for the filtered output, we can understand why this produces the infinite impulse response. For the EMA, this is

$$Y(z) = H(z)X(z)$$
$$= \frac{\alpha X(z)}{1 - (1 - \alpha)z^{-1}}$$

When we multiply both sides of this equation by the denominator on the right side, we obtain

$$Y(z) - (1 - \alpha)Y(z)z^{-1} = \alpha X(z)$$
$$Y(z) = \alpha X(z) + (1 - \alpha)Y(z)z^{-1}$$

This equation says that the current output depends not only on the current input, but also on the output one sample ago. That is, the calculation is recursive. This repeats for each subsequent sample, so that the current output always depends on all previous outputs.

The IIR filters are generally patterned after specific analog filter shapes such as Butterworth, Chebyshev, or Elliptic designs. Scaling and accuracy considerations are much more important for IIR filters than for FIR filters because the iterative calculations compound rounding errors, and good judgment must be used to determine if a particular filter is practical given the number of bits available. We must give special attention to limit cycles, which are low-level oscillations due to rounding error in computation. As rounding errors are included in each recursion, the results can be cumulative. This kind of error causes particular trouble when using EasyLanguage because TradeStation rounds floating point calculations to 4 bits. If an IIR filter blows up on you, the problem may not be a bug in your code, but may result from limit cycles. If this occurs, you must modify the design. One thing you can do is compute the filter response in a Dynamic Linked Library (DLL) that has been compiled at a higher level of precision, and call up that DLL from your Easy-Language code.

A *pole* is a zero of the denominator polynomial of a filter transfer response. The EMA has a single pole in its transfer response. More complex filters use a larger number of samples of previous outputs, and therefore have a higher-order polynomial in the denominator of the transfer response. From the

fundamental theorem of algebra, we know that this polynomial can be factored into zeros of the polynomial. Since the
polynomial is in the denominator of the transfer response,
these factors are called the poles of the response. These are the
values of z^{-1} at which the transfer response blows up mathematically because the denominator is zero, giving an infinite
result. This cannot happen in the filters because z^{-1} is constrained to be in integer numbers and the poles never occur at
integer numbers in stable filters. Higher-order filters are called
multipole filters. In trading, we are limited to just a few poles to
calculate IIR responses because each pole necessarily brings
additional lag. Without the lag consideration, we could theoretically continue to add an infinite number of poles to our filter
design to create a stone-wall filter response at the critical period.

Butterworth Filters

There is a host of multipole filter designs available. One of the
more common multipole filter responses is called a *Butterworth filter*. This filter is maximally smooth at zero frequency.
That is, it has the highest number of derivatives that have a null
value at zero frequency. The filtering advantage of using multipole Butterworth filters is shown in the comparison in Figure
15.1. All three filters have a cutoff period at a 20-bar cycle. We
clearly get more filtering with each increase in the number of
poles.

The low-frequency lag of Butterworth filters can be computed by the following equation:

$$\text{Lag} = N * P / \pi^2$$

where N = number of poles in the filter
         P = critical period of the filter

The equations for a two-pole Butterworth filter in EasyLanguage
notation are

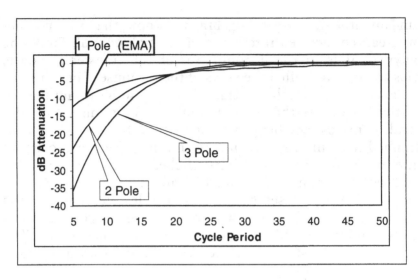

Figure 15.1. Comparison of Butterworth filters that have a 20-bar cutoff period.

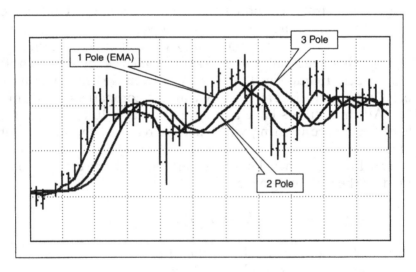

Figure 15.2. Responses for one-, two-, and three-pole filters having a 14-bar cutoff. Increasing the number of poles increases the lag for a common cutoff period.

Chart created with TradeStation2000i® by Omega Research, Inc.

$a = \text{ExpValue}(-1.414*3.14159/P);$

$b = 2*a*\text{Cos}\ (1.414*180/P);$

$y = b*y[1] - a*a*y[2] + ((1 - b + a*a)/4)*(x + 2*x[1] + x[2]);$

where P = cutoff period of the two-pole filter. The equations for a three-pole Butterworth filter in EasyLanguage notation are

$a = \text{ExpValue}(-3.14159/P);$

$b = 2*a*\text{Cos}\ (1.738*180/P);$

$c = a*a;$

$y = (b + c)*y[1] - (c + b*c)*y[2] + c*c*y[3]$
$\quad + ((1 - b + c)*(1 - c)/8)*(x + 3*x[1] + 3*x[2] + x[3]);$

where P = cutoff period of the three-pole filter. The merits of the higher-order filters are shown in Figures 15.2 and 15.3. Clearly, the higher-order filters offer greater fidelity when the lag is held constant.

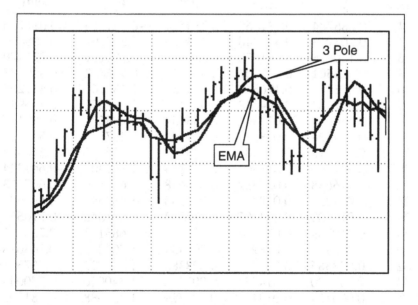

Figure 15.3.   One- and three-pole filter responses when equalized for a 2-bar lag. The higher order filter has greater fidelity when the lag is held constant.

Chart created with TradeStation2000i® by Omega Research, Inc.

Butterworth Filter Tables

It is often easier to use a lookup table to get filter coefficients than uniquely calculate the coefficients each time they are used. In Tables 15.1 and 15.2, the notation is defined as follows: A[0] is used with the current price data, A[n] is used with the price data [n] bars ago, A[2] is used with price data 2 bars ago, and B[n] is used with the previously calculated filter output [n] bars ago. These tables are sure to make it easier to use higher-order filters.

Gaussian and Other Low-Lag Filters

The first objective of using smoothers is to eliminate or reduce the undesired high-frequency components in the price data.

Table 15.1. Two-Pole Butterworth Filter Coefficients

Period	A[0]	A[1]	A[2]	B[1]	B[2]
2	0.285784	0.571568	0.285784	−0.131366	−0.011770
4	0.203973	0.407946	0.203973	0.292597	−0.108489
6	0.130825	0.261650	0.130825	0.704171	−0.227470
8	0.088501	0.177002	0.088501	0.975372	−0.329377
10	0.063284	0.126567	0.063284	1.158161	−0.411296
12	0.047322	0.094643	0.047322	1.287652	−0.476938
14	0.036654	0.073308	0.036654	1.383531	−0.530147
16	0.029198	0.058397	0.029198	1.457120	−0.573914
18	0.023793	0.047586	0.023793	1.515266	−0.610438
20	0.019754	0.039507	0.019754	1.562309	−0.641324
22	0.016658	0.033317	0.016658	1.601119	−0.667753
24	0.014235	0.028470	0.014235	1.633667	−0.690607
26	0.012303	0.024607	0.012303	1.661342	−0.710555
28	0.010739	0.021477	0.010739	1.685157	−0.728112
30	0.009454	0.018908	0.009454	1.705862	−0.743678
32	0.008386	0.016773	0.008386	1.724025	−0.757571
34	0.007490	0.014980	0.007490	1.740086	−0.770045
36	0.006729	0.013459	0.006729	1.754388	−0.781305
38	0.006079	0.012158	0.006079	1.767204	−0.791520
40	0.005518	0.011037	0.005518	1.778753	−0.800827

Table 15.2. Three-Pole Butterworth Filter Coefficients

Period	A[0]	A[1]	A[2]	A[3]	B[1]	B[2]	B[3]
2	0.170149	0.510448	0.510448	0.170149	-0.336246	-0.026816	0.001867
4	0.100733	0.302200	0.302200	0.100733	0.398405	-0.247486	0.043214
6	0.050373	0.151118	0.151118	0.050373	1.080990	-0.607116	0.123145
8	0.027610	0.082830	0.082830	0.027610	1.505892	-0.934652	0.207880
10	0.016541	0.049622	0.049622	0.016541	1.783327	-1.200263	0.284610
12	0.010629	0.031887	0.031887	0.010629	1.976163	-1.412114	0.350920
14	0.007213	0.021640	0.021640	0.007213	2.117205	-1.582459	0.407548
16	0.005111	0.015334	0.015334	0.005111	2.224560	-1.721388	0.455938
18	0.003750	0.011250	0.011250	0.003750	2.308883	-1.836396	0.497514
20	0.002831	0.008492	0.008492	0.002831	2.376806	-1.932941	0.533488
22	0.002188	0.006565	0.006565	0.002188	2.432658	-2.015013	0.564848
24	0.001726	0.005179	0.005179	0.001726	2.479376	-2.085571	0.592385
26	0.001385	0.004156	0.004156	0.001385	2.519020	-2.146834	0.616731
28	0.001128	0.003385	0.003385	0.001128	2.553078	-2.200500	0.638395
30	0.000931	0.002794	0.002794	0.000931	2.582648	-2.247883	0.657784
32	0.000778	0.002333	0.002333	0.000778	2.608560	-2.290012	0.675232
34	0.000656	0.001967	0.001967	0.000656	2.631451	-2.327708	0.691011
36	0.000558	0.001674	0.001674	0.000558	2.651819	-2.361631	0.705347
38	0.000479	0.001437	0.001437	0.000479	2.670059	-2.392315	0.718425
40	0.000414	0.001242	0.001242	0.000414	2.686486	-2.420202	0.730403

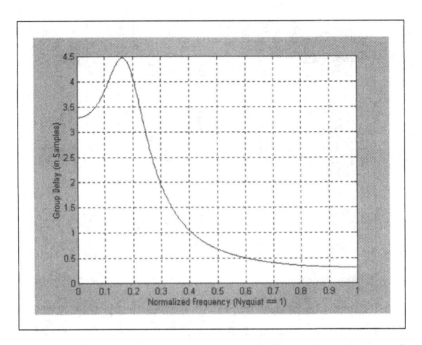

Figure 15.4. Lag of a three-pole Butterworth filter with a 10-bar period cutoff.

Therefore, these smoothers are called *low-pass filters*, and they all work by some form of averaging. Butterworth low-pass filters can do this job, but nothing comes for free. A higher degree of filtering is necessarily accompanied by a larger amount of lag. We have come to see that this is a fact of life.

The downfall of most trading indicators, lag causes the failure to react to price changes in a timely manner. A better approach to filtering, therefore, is to minimize the lag and accept the resultant smoothing. The importance of lag (group delay is an engineer's way of saying lag, which distinguishes lag from the phase delay through the filter) is demonstrated in Figure 15.4. This illustrates the lag of a three-pole Butterworth filter that attenuates cycles shorter than 10 bars.

The low-frequency lag of a Butterworth filter can be estimated by the following equation, where N is the number of poles in the filter and P is the longest cycle period to pass through the filter:

$$\text{Lag} = N^*P/\pi^2$$

The lag story gets worse as the frequency components of the input waveform get closer to the band edge of the filter. The higher-frequency components within the passband of the filter are actually delayed *more* than the lower-frequency components. This is exactly the opposite of what a trader desires. We have to react more quickly to rapid changes in the market, and we therefore prefer a smoothing filter that has less lag with the higher-frequency components.

A *Gaussian filter* is one whose transfer response is described by the familiar Gaussian bell-shaped curve. In the case of low-pass filters, only the upper half of the curve describes the filter. The use of Gaussian filters is a move toward achieving the dual goals of reducing lag and reducing the lag of high-frequency components relative to the lag of lower-frequency components. We can construct multipole Gaussian filters that provide a desired degree of smoothing. The group delay of a three-pole Gaussian filter having a 0.1 cycle per day passband is shown in Figure 15.5 for comparison to the delay produced by a Butterworth filter.

For an equivalent number of poles, the lag of a Gaussian filter is about half the lag of a Butterworth filter. More important, the higher-frequency components have even less lag than the low-frequency components. With Gaussian filters, the lag (as a function of frequency) goes in the right direction for traders—decreased lag. However, a Gaussian filter has about half the smoothing effectiveness as an equivalently sized Butterworth filter. A four-pole Gaussian filter has about the same smoothing performance as a two-pole Butterworth filter. Thus, performing the same amount of filtering, these two filters have about the same low-frequency lag, but the Gaussian filter preserves the original price function with greater fidelity because the higher-frequency components within the passband are not delayed as much as those within the Butterworth filter. Comparative filter responses of a two-pole Butterworth filter and a two-pole Gaussian filter, each having a 10-bar cycle passband, are shown in Figure 15.6.

There is no magic to the Gaussian filter. It can be defined simply as the multiple application of an Exponential Moving Average (EMA). The transfer response of an EMA is

$$H(z) = \frac{\alpha}{1 - (1 - \alpha)z^{-1}}$$

Applying the EMA N times gives us an N-pole Gaussian filter transfer response expressed by the following equation:

$$H(z) = \left(\frac{\alpha}{1 - (1 - \alpha)z^{-1}} \right)^N$$

At zero frequency, $z^{-1} = 1$ because the Z Transform of a function is just the function itself at zero frequency. Therefore, this low-pass filter gain is unity. Also, the denominator assumes the value of α^N at zero frequency. The cutoff frequency of the filter is defined as that point where the transfer response is down by 3 dB, or 0.707 in amplitude. If the transfer response is down by 3 dB, then the denominator, the only term that is a function of

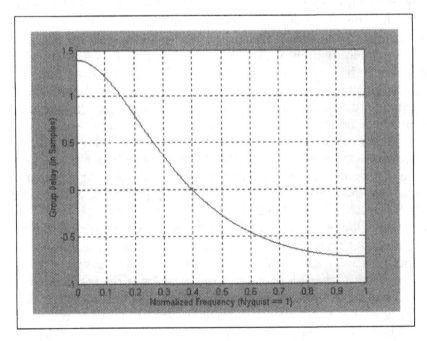

Figure 15.5.   Lag of a three-pole Gaussian filter with a 10-bar period cutoff.

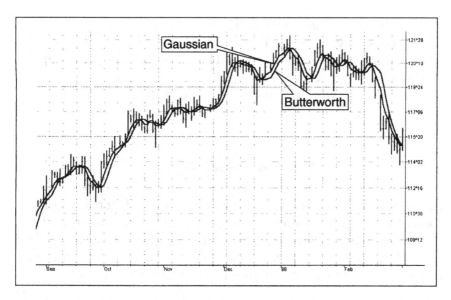

Figure 15.6 Comparison of two-pole filters illustrates that the Gaussian filter has much less lag than the Butterworth filter. The Gaussian filter has less smoothing.
Chart created with TradeStation2000i® by Omega Research, Inc.

frequency, must be up by 3 dB, or 1.414 in amplitude. When this occurs, we obtain the following relationship:

$$(1 - (1 - \alpha)z^{-1})^N = 1.414\alpha^N$$

where $z^{-1} = e^{-j\omega}$ and $\omega = 2\pi/P$. Crunching through the complex arithmetic, we arrive at the solution for alpha as

$$\alpha = -\beta + \text{SQR}(\beta^2 + 2\beta)$$

where $\beta = (1 - \cos(\omega))/(1.414^{2/N} - 1)$.

We can use this generalized solution for alpha to compute the coefficients for any order Gaussian filter. And, because z^{-1} is synonymous with a 1-bar lag, we can easily use EasyLanguage code to form equations from the N-pole transfer response for the output.

One pole: $y = \alpha x + (1 - \alpha)y[1]$
Two poles: $y = \alpha^2 x + 2(1 - \alpha)y[1] - (1 - \alpha)^2 y[2]$
Three poles: $y = \alpha^3 x + 3(1 - \alpha)y[1] - 3(1 - \alpha)^2 y[2] + (1 - \alpha)^3 y[3]$
Four poles: $y = \alpha^4 x + 4(1 - \alpha)y[1] - 6(1 - \alpha)^2 y[2]$
$$+ 4(1 - \alpha)^3 y[3] - (1 - \alpha)^4 y[4]$$

$$\vdots$$

Gaussian Filter Tables

As we have seen in terms of the Butterworth filter, it is often easier to consult a lookup table to get filter coefficients than it is to calculate the coefficients each time they are used. In Tables 15.3–15.6, column A lists the price data coefficient and column B lists the previously calculated filter output [n] bars ago.

Table 15.3.   One-Pole Gaussian Filter (EMA)

Period	A[0]	B[1]
2	0.828427	0.171573
4	0.732051	0.267949
6	0.618034	0.381966
8	0.526602	0.473398
10	0.455887	0.544113
12	0.400720	0.599280
14	0.356896	0.643104
16	0.321416	0.678584
18	0.292186	0.707814
20	0.267730	0.732270
22	0.246990	0.753010
24	0.229192	0.770808
26	0.213760	0.786240
28	0.200256	0.799744
30	0.188343	0.811657
32	0.177759	0.822241
34	0.168294	0.831706
36	0.159780	0.840220
38	0.152082	0.847918
40	0.145089	0.854911

Table 15.4. Two-Pole Gaussian Filter Coefficients

Period	A[0]	B[1]	B[2]
2	0.834615	0.172854	−0.007470
4	0.722959	0.299460	−0.022419
6	0.578300	0.479080	−0.057379
8	0.457577	0.647112	−0.104688
10	0.365017	0.791668	−0.156684
12	0.295336	0.913103	−0.208439
14	0.242632	1.014847	−0.257479
16	0.202250	1.100556	−0.302806
18	0.170835	1.173357	−0.344192
20	0.146017	1.235757	−0.381774
22	0.126125	1.289719	−0.415844
24	0.109966	1.336777	−0.446743
26	0.096680	1.378133	−0.474813
28	0.085633	1.414738	−0.500371
30	0.076357	1.447346	−0.523703
32	0.068496	1.476567	−0.545063
34	0.061779	1.502894	−0.564672
36	0.055996	1.526729	−0.582726
38	0.050984	1.548408	−0.599392
40	0.046612	1.568205	−0.614817

Table 15.5.   Three-Pole Gaussian Filter Coefficients

Period	A[0]	B[1]	B[2]	B[3]
2	0.836701	0.173094	−0.009987	0.000192
4	0.718670	0.312814	−0.032617	0.001134
6	0.558792	0.529009	−0.093283	0.005483
8	0.422292	0.749259	−0.187130	0.015579
10	0.318295	0.951680	−0.301899	0.031923
12	0.242068	1.130321	−0.425875	0.053486
14	0.186612	1.285644	−0.550960	0.078704
16	0.146016	1.420251	−0.672371	0.106104
18	0.115940	1.537154	−0.787614	0.134520
20	0.093340	1.639147	−0.895601	0.163114
22	0.076111	1.728632	−0.996056	0.191313
24	0.062791	1.807607	−1.089148	0.218750
26	0.052354	1.877714	−1.175270	0.245202
28	0.044075	1.940297	−1.254918	0.270546
30	0.037432	1.996460	−1.328618	0.294726
32	0.032045	2.047111	−1.396887	0.317731
34	0.027635	2.093000	−1.460217	0.339582
36	0.023991	2.134754	−1.519058	0.360313
38	0.020956	2.172895	−1.573824	0.379973
40	0.018409	2.207865	−1.624889	0.398615

Table 15.6.   Four-Pole Gaussian Filter Coefficients

Period	A[0]	B[1]	B[2]	B[3]	B[4]
2	0.837747	0.173178	−0.011247	0.000325	0.000004
4	0.716200	0.320247	−0.038459	0.002053	0.000041
6	0.547128	0.559812	−0.117521	0.010965	0.000384
8	0.400596	0.817734	−0.250758	0.034176	0.001747
10	0.289459	1.066023	−0.426152	0.075715	0.005045
12	0.209659	1.293310	−0.627244	0.135204	0.010929
14	0.153408	1.496649	−0.839984	0.209527	0.019599
16	0.113779	1.676861	−1.054449	0.294694	0.030885
18	0.085632	1.836187	−1.264344	0.386929	0.044405
20	0.065397	1.977213	−1.466015	0.483104	0.059700
22	0.050648	2.102418	−1.657560	0.580814	0.076320
24	0.039744	2.214012	−1.838193	0.678297	0.093860
26	0.031571	2.313903	−2.007804	0.774311	0.111980
28	0.025363	2.403709	−2.166681	0.868012	0.130403
30	0.020589	2.484797	−2.315331	0.958854	0.148910
32	0.016875	2.558316	−2.454368	1.046508	0.167331
34	0.013953	2.625237	−2.584450	1.130799	0.185538
36	0.011632	2.686378	−2.706235	1.211662	0.203436
38	0.009770	2.742435	−2.820356	1.289107	0.220956
40	0.008263	2.794000	−2.927413	1.363199	0.238049

Key Points to Remember

- An Exponential Moving Average (EMA) is an Infinite Impulse Response (IIR) filter, having only one pole in its response.
- Classical filter types, such as Butterworth, Chebyshev, and Gaussian are IIR filters.
- Lag of an IIR filter is nonlinear as a function of input frequency.
- Low-frequency lag of a Butterworth filter is $N*P/\pi^2$.
- Gaussian filters have the least lag of all the multipole filters. The low-frequency lag is approximately half the low-frequency lag of an equivalently sized Butterworth filter.
- Calculations involving IIR filters can blow up due to the cumulative effect of rounding errors in the computation.

Chapter 16

REMOVING LAG

*Money is a terrible master
but an excellent servant.*

—P.T. Barnum

In 1960, R.E. Kalman introduced the concept of optimum estimation. Since then, his technique has proven to be a powerful and practical tool. The approach it utilizes is particularly well-suited for optimizing the performance of modern terrestrial and space navigation systems. Many traders not directly involved in system analysis have heard about Kalman filtering and have expressed interest in learning more about applying it to the market. Although attempts have been made to provide simple, intuitive explanations, none has been completely successful. Almost without exception, descriptions have become mired in the jargon and state-space notation of the cult.

In spite of the obscure-looking mathematics (the most impenetrable of which can be found in Dr. Kalman's original paper), Kalman filtering is a surprisingly direct and simple concept. In the spirit of pragmatism, we will not deal with the full-blown matrix equations that a thorough explanation of Kalman filtering requires, and we will be less than rigorous in its application to trading. Rigorous application requires knowledge of the probability distributions of the statistics. Nonetheless, we end with practical and useful results. We depart from the classical approach by working backward from Exponential Moving Averages (EMAs). With this process, we introduce a method to achieve a nearly zero-lag moving average. From there, we develop an automatic trading system based on the zero-lag principle.

Suboptimal Filters

Tracking filters use a linear model to estimate the position of a target. The classic example is a gunner shooting at an enemy target. He estimates the angle of his gun and shoots. The forward foot soldiers radio back how much deviation there was from the target. The gunner computes the incremental change required for his new gun angle from the deviation. An Alpha filter shows that this model constitutes using the previous estimate plus a constant times the difference between the last real position and the last estimate. The equation for this filter is

$$X^\wedge = X^\wedge[1] + \alpha(Z - X^\wedge[1])$$

where $X^\wedge$ = estimated next position
Z = last real position

This is exactly the same as the EMA with which you are familiar. Let us rearrange the terms so that the EMA is written as

$$\text{EMA} = \alpha*\text{Price} + (1 - \alpha)*\text{EMA}[1]$$

As you know, this EMA equation produces a lag in the estimated price. We can improve our estimate of position by adding an estimate of the velocity to the last known position. The position equation then becomes

$$X^\wedge = X^\wedge[1] + \alpha((Z + K*V^\wedge) - X^\wedge[1])$$

where $V^\wedge$ = velocity estimate
K = gain factor

The velocity estimate is an EMA of the rate of change of position, so that

$$V^{\wedge} = V^{\wedge}[1] + \beta(V - V^{\wedge}[1])$$

This is the Beta part of an Alpha-Beta filter. An Alpha-Beta filter considers not only the change of position, but also the change of velocity. In trading terms, an Alpha-Beta filter not only considers the price, but also the change of price (momentum).

We can create a near-zero-lag filter for the special case where $\beta = 1$. In this case, the EMA can be written as

$$\text{ZEMA} = \alpha^{*}(\text{Price} + K^{*}(\text{Price} - \text{Price}[3])) + (1 - \alpha)^{*}\text{ZEMA}[1]$$

where ZEMA is the zero-lag EMA. I took the liberty of using the three-day momentum as the velocity estimate. Figure 16.1 shows

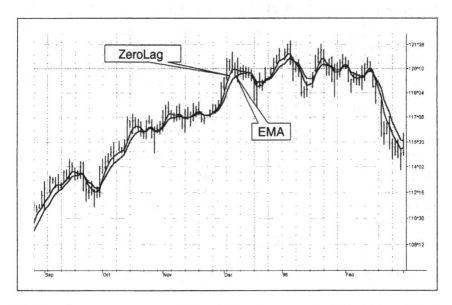

Figure 16.1. ZeroLag moving average compared to standard EMA with $\alpha = 0.25$.
Chart created with TradeStation2000i® by Omega Research, Inc.

an EMA using α = 0.25 compared to a ZEMA using the same alpha and K = 0.5. This is not a bad zero-lag filter, even if it is suboptimal. It is suboptimal because it is not a true Kalman filter.

ZeroLag Trading System

The concepts of the Instantaneous Trendline and the ZeroLag EMA are very powerful. To demonstrate just how profound these concepts are, I designed an intraday trading system and applied it to one of the more exciting and challenging contracts that exist today—the S&P futures. An *intraday trade* is defined as any active trade that is traded and then closed at the end of the day. Figure 16.2 illustrates the back-tested results of the S&P futures

Total Net Profit	$146,450.00		
Gross Profit	$336,937.50	Gross Loss	($190,487.50)
Total # of trades	283	Percent profitable	50.18%
Number winning trades	142	Number losing trades	141
Largest winning trade	$15,000.00	Largest losing trade	($1,512.50)
Average winning trade	$2,372.80	Average losing trade	($1,350.98)
Ratio avg win/ avg loss	1.76	Avg trade (win & loss)	$517.49
Max consec. Winners	7	Max consec. losers	9
Avg # bars in winners	7	Avg # bars in losers	4
Max intraday drawdown	($17,650.00)		
Profit Factor	1.77	Max # contracts held	1

Figure 16.2. ZeroLag performance summary on S&P intraday—1 January 1997 to 7 June 2000.

market from 1 January 1997 to 7 June 2000. A $1,500 money-management stop was used. The results included an average income over $40,000 per year per contract at an average profit per trade of $517, and slightly more than half of all trades were profitable! This system trades an average of 1.5 times a week. The new part of the code (after the Hilbert calculations, with which you are familiar) starts where I set yesterday's high and low, computed by sequentially capturing the highest high and the lowest low today. The ZEMA is computed using a gain factor of 0.5. Now the trading rules come into play.

Rule number one demands an outside day for any trade to be taken. That is, either the highest high today must be higher than yesterday's high or the lowest low today must be lower than yesterday's low. Next, a new position is entered only on the second bar of the day. A new position is established by the condition that the MarketPosition equals zero (Flat Position). Then, on the second bar of the day, if the ZeroLag line is above the Instantaneous Trendline and the filter conditions are met, a long position is established. The filter conditions are as follows: The open of the second bar must be greater than the open of the first; the high of the second bar must be higher than the high of the first; and the close of the first bar must be in the upper two-thirds of its range. A similar rule exists for the short side trade. That is, the open of the second bar must be less than the open of the first; the low of the second bar must be lower than the low of the first; and the close of the first bar must be in the lower two-thirds of its range. Also, a crossover rule exists for all bars. If you find that the following set of conditions is met, then buy: The ZeroLag crosses over the Instantaneous Trendline, the high of the current bar is less than the high of the previous one, and the close of the current bar is in the upper half of the range of the bar. If this set of conditions is met, then sell: The ZeroLag crosses under the Instantaneous Trendline, the low of the current bar is greater than the low of the previous one, and the close of the current bar is in the lower half of the range of the bar.

The complete code to achieve this performance is given in Figure 16.3. There is not a lot of new code. The majority of the code is used to compute the Instantaneous Trendline. We use an

```
Inputs: Price((H+L)/2),
        alpha(.33);

Vars: Smooth(0),
      Detrender(0),
      I1(0),
      Q1(0),
      jI(0),
      jQ(0),
      I2(0),
      Q2(0),
      Re(0),
      Im(0),
      Period(0),
      SmoothPeriod(0),
      SmoothPrice(0),
      DCPeriod(0),
      RealPart(0),
      ImagPart(0),
      count(0),
      ITrend(0),
      Trendline(0),
      ZeroLag(0),
      Ht(0),
      Lt(0),
      Yh(0),
      Y1(0);

      {Initialize ZeroLag}
      If CurrentBar = 5 then begin
            ZeroLag = (H+L)/2;
      End;

If CurrentBar > 5 then begin
      Smooth = (4*Price + 3*Price[1] + 2*Price[2] +
        Price[3]) / 10;
      Detrender = (.0962*Smooth + .5769*Smooth[2] -
        .5769*Smooth[4] - .0962*Smooth[6])*(.075*
        Period[1] + .54);
                                        (continued)
```

Figure 16.3. ZeroLag Intraday Trading System EasyLanguage code.

```
{Compute InPhase and Quadrature components}
Q1 = (.0962*Detrender + .5769*Detrender[2] -
  .5769*Detrender[4] - .0962*Detrender[6])*
  (.075*Period[1] + .54);
I1 = Detrender[3];

{Advance the phase of I1 and Q1 by 90 degrees}
jI = (.0962*I1 + .5769*I1[2] - .5769*I1[4] -
  .0962*I1[6])*(.075*Period[1] + .54);
jQ = (.0962*Q1 + .5769*Q1[2] - .5769*Q1[4] -
  .0962*Q1[6])*(.075*Period[1] + .54);

{Phasor addition for 3 bar averaging)}
I2 = I1 - jQ;
Q2 = Q1 + jI;

{Smooth the I and Q components before applying
  the discriminator}
I2 = .2*I2 + .8*I2[1];
Q2 = .2*Q2 + .8*Q2[1];

{Homodyne Discriminator}
Re = I2*I2[1] + Q2*Q2[1];
Im = I2*Q2[1] - Q2*I2[1];
Re = .2*Re + .8*Re[1];
Im = .2*Im + .8*Im[1];
If Im <> 0 and Re <> 0 then Period =
  360/ArcTangent(Im/Re);
If Period > 1.5*Period[1] then Period =
  1.5*Period[1];
If Period < .67*Period[1] then Period =
  .67*Period[1];
If Period < 6 then Period = 6;
If Period > 50 then Period = 50;
Period = .2*Period + .8*Period[1];
SmoothPeriod = .33*Period + .67*SmoothPeriod[1];

{Compute Trendline as simple average over the
  measured dominant cycle period}
DCPeriod = IntPortion(SmoothPeriod + .5);
```

(continued)

Figure 16.3. *(Continued)*.

```
ITrend = 0;
For count = 0 to DCPeriod - 1 begin
    ITrend = ITrend + Price[count];
End;
If DCPeriod > 0 then ITrend = ITrend / DCPeriod;
Trendline = (4*ITrend + 3*ITrend[1] + 2*
  ITrend[2] + ITrend[3]) / 10;
If CurrentBar < 12 then Trendline = Price;

{Set yesterday's high and low}
If Date <> Date[1] then begin
    Ht = High;
    Lt = Low;
    Yh = Ht[1];
    Yl = Lt[1];
End;

{Establish today's high and low}
If High > Ht then Ht = High;
If Low < Lt then Lt = Low;

{Compute zero lag filter}
ZeroLag = alpha*(Price + .5*(Price - Price[3])) +
  (1 - alpha)*ZeroLag[1];

{Demand an outside day to trade}
If Date >= 0 and (Ht >= Yh or Lt <= Yl) then
  begin
      {New positions are entered at the end of
        the second bar of the day}
      If Date = Date[1] and Date > Date[2] and
      MarketPosition = 0 then begin
          If ZeroLag > Trendline and Open >
          Open[1] and High > High[1] and
          Close[1] > Low[1] + (High[1] -
          Low[1])/ 3 then buy;
          If ZeroLag < Trendline and Open <
          Open[1] and Low < Low[1] and
          Close[1] < High[1] - (High[1] -
          Low[1])/ 3 then sell;
      End;
                                    (continued)
```

Figure 16.3.   (*Continued*).

```
        If ZeroLag Crosses Over Trendline and High
           < High[1] and Close > Low + (High -
           Low)/2 then buy;
        If ZeroLag Crosses Under Trendline and Low
           > Low[1] and Close > High - (High -
           Low)/2 then sell;
     End;
End;
```

Figure 16.3. (*Continued*).

additional input—the alpha used in the ZeroLag EMA. In this case, I assigned a value of 0.33 to alpha, corresponding to a 2-bar lag if the EMA lag was not removed.

Key Points to Remember

- Exponential Moving Average (EMA) lag can be removed by adding a short-term momentum factor times a gain term to the current price in the EMA equation.
- A ZeroLag EMA is similar to a Kalman filter with a constant gain.
- The theoretical Instantaneous Trendline and ZeroLag Indicators are powerful tools even for demanding intraday trading.

Chapter 17

MAMA—THE MOTHER OF ADAPTIVE MOVING AVERAGES

*Think like a man of action,
act like a man of thought.*

—HENRI-LOUIS BERGSON

We have already encountered one method to make Finite Impulse Response (FIR) filters adaptive—setting the cutoff frequency to be some multiplier times the measured cycle period. In certain special cases, the length of the Simple Moving Average (SMA) is set not only to smooth, but also to specifically notch out, some undesired frequency components. The Instantaneous Trendline is one such example. We can produce a much faster response to changes if we introduce nonlinearity into an Infinite Impulse Response (IIR) filter calculation. Nonlinearities usually depend on price volatility. We briefly describe several of these approaches before applying the Hilbert Transform for a unique approach.

Kaufman's Adaptive Moving Average

Kaufman's Adaptive Moving Average (KAMA) is based on the concept that a noisy market requires a slower trend than one

with less noise.[1] The basic principle is that the trendline must
lag further behind the price in a relatively noisy market to avoid
being penetrated by the price. The moving average can speed up
when the prices move consistently in one direction. According
to Perry Kaufman, who invented the system, KAMA is intended
to use the fastest trend possible, based on the smallest calculation period for the existing market conditions. It does this by
changing the alpha of the EMA with each new sample. The
equation for KAMA is

$$KAMA = S*Price + (1 - S)*KAMA[1]$$

where S = smoothing factor. This is exactly the same equation
that we use for the Exponential Moving Average (EMA) except
the variable S replaces the alpha constant of the EMA.

The equation for the smoothing factor involves two boundaries and an efficiency ratio.

$$S = (E*(fastest - slowest) + slowest)^2$$

Fastest refers to the alpha of the shortest period boundary. Slowest refers to the alpha of the longest period boundary. The suggested period boundaries are 2 and 30 bars. In this case, the two
alphas are calculated to be

$$Fastest = 2/(2 + 1) = 0.6667$$
$$Slowest = 2/(30 + 1) = 0.0645$$

Simplifying the equation for the smoothing factor, we get

$$S = (0.6022*E + 0.0645)^2$$

The *efficiency ratio* (E) is the absolute value of the difference
of price across the calculation span divided by the sum of the

[1]Kaufman, Perry J. *Trading Systems and Methods*. 3rd ed. New York:
John Wiley & Sons, 1998.

absolute value of the individual price differences across the calculation span. The equation for E is

$$E = \frac{|\text{Price} - \text{Price}[N]|}{\sum\limits_{i=0}^{N} |\text{Price}[i] - \text{Price}[i+1]|}$$

The default value for N is 10. However, testing to find the best length is suggested.

Variable Index Dynamic Average

Variable Index Dynamic Average (VIDYA) uses a pivotal smoothing constant that is fixed.[2] The suggested value of this constant is 0.2, corresponding to the alpha of a nine-day EMA. The equation for VIDYA is

$$\text{VIDYA} = 0.2 {}^* k {}^* \text{Close} + (1 - 0.2 {}^* k) {}^* \text{VIDYA}[1]$$

Again, this is exactly the same equation as an EMA except the relative volatility term k has been included to introduce the nonlinearity. The *volatility term* is the ratio of the standard deviation of Closes over the last n days to the standard deviation of Closes over the last m days, where m is greater than n. Suggested values are $n = 9$ and $m = 30$.

MESA Adaptive Moving Average—a.k.a. MAMA

Forgive the whimsy of the name I attached to this unique indicator, but with that name I'm sure you will always remember it. Like KAMA and VIDYA, the starting point for MAMA is a con-

---

[2]Chande, Tushar S., and Stanley Kroll. *The New Technical Trader.* New York: John Wiley & Sons, 1994.

ventional Exponential Moving Average (EMA). The equation for an EMA is written as

$$EMA = \alpha * Price + (1 - \alpha) * EMA[1]$$

where α is less than 1. In English, this equation says that the EMA is comprised of taking a fraction of the current price and adding one minus that fraction times the previous value of the EMA. The larger the value of α, the more responsive the EMA becomes to the current price. Conversely, if α becomes smaller, the EMA is more dependent on previous values of the average rather than the current price. Therefore, a way to make an EMA adaptive is to vary the value of α according to some independent parameter.

The concept of MAMA is to relate the phase rate of change to the EMA alpha, thus making the EMA adaptive. The cycle phase goes from 0 through 360 degrees in each cycle. The phase is continuous, but is usually drawn with the snap back to 0 degrees as the beginning of each cycle. Thus the phase rate of change is 360 degrees per cycle. The shorter the cycle, the faster the phase rate of change. For example, a 36-bar cycle has a phase rate of change of 10 degrees per bar, while a 10-bar cycle has a rate of change of 36 degrees per bar. The cycle periods tend to be longer when the market is in a Trend Mode.

The cycle phase is computed from the arctangent of the ratio of the Quadrature component to the InPhase component. I obtain the phase rate of change values by taking the difference of successive phase measurements. The arctangent function only measures phase over a half cycle, from –90 degrees to +90 degrees. Since the phase measurement snaps back every half cycle, a huge negative rate change of phase every half cycle results from the computation of the rate change of phase. Measured negative rate changes of phase can also occur when the market is in a Trend Mode. Any negative rate change of phase is theoretically impossible because phase must advance as time increases. We therefore limit all rate change of phase to be no less than unity.

The alpha in MAMA is allowed to range between a maximum and minimum value, these values being established as inputs. The suggested maximum value is FastLimit = 0.5, and the suggested minimum is SlowLimit = 0.05. The variable alpha is computed as the FastLimit divided by the phase rate of change. Any time there is a negative phase rate of change, the value of alpha is set to the FastLimit. If the phase rate of change is large, the variable alpha is bounded at the SlowLimit.

The arctangent function produces a phase response between −90 degrees and +90 degrees, with a phase wrap back to −90 degrees. There is a huge negative rate change of phase across this phase wrap boundary. By limiting this negative rate change of phase to +1, the alpha used in the EMA is set to the FastLimit. The phase wrap boundary occurs at 0 degrees and 180 degrees of a theoretical sine wave due to the 90-degree lag of the Hilbert Transform.

The variable alpha is guaranteed to be set to the FastLimit every half cycle due to the measured phase snap back. This relatively large value of alpha causes MAMA to rapidly approach the price. After the phase snaps back, the alpha returns to a typically small value. The small value of alpha causes MAMA to hold nearly the value it achieved when alpha was at the FastLimit. This switching between the relatively large and relatively small values of alpha produce the ratcheting action that you observe in the waveform. The ratcheting occurs less often when the market is in the Trend Mode because the cycle period is longer in these cases.

An interesting set of indicators result if the MAMA is applied to the first MAMA line to produce a Following Adaptive Moving Average (FAMA). By using an alpha in FAMA that is half the value of the alpha in MAMA, the FAMA has steps in time synchronization with MAMA, but the vertical movement is not as great. As a result, MAMA and FAMA do not cross unless there has been a major change in market direction. This suggests an adaptive moving average crossover system that is virtually free of whipsaw trades.

The MAMA code is shown in Figure 17.1. This code is nearly the same as the one that computes the Hilbert Transform Homodyne Discriminator cycle measurement (see Chapter 7, Figure 7.2), with the additional code to compute phase rate of change, the nonlinear alpha, and the MAMA and FAMA lines.

```
Inputs:        Price((H+L)/2),
               FastLimit(.5),
               SlowLimit(.05);

Vars:  Smooth(0),
       Detrender(0),
       I1(0),
       Q1(0),
       jI(0),
       jQ(0),
       I2(0),
       Q2(0),
       Re(0),
       Im(0),
       Period(0),
       SmoothPeriod(0),
       Phase(0),
       DeltaPhase(0),
       alpha(0),
       MAMA(0);
       FAMA(0);

If CurrentBar > 5 then begin
       Smooth = (4*Price + 3*Price[1] + 2*Price[2] +
       Price[3]) / 10;
       Detrender = (.0962*Smooth + .5769*Smooth[2] -
       .5769*Smooth[4] - .0962*Smooth[6])*
       (.075*Period[1] + .54);

       {Compute InPhase and Quadrature components}
       Q1 = (.0962*Detrender + .5769*Detrender[2] -
       .5769*Detrender[4] - .0962*Detrender[6])*
       (.075*Period[1] + .54);
       I1 = Detrender[3];

       {Advance the phase of I1 and Q1 by 90 degrees}
       jI = (.0962*I1 + .5769*I1[2] - .5769*I1[4] -
       .0962*I1[6])*(.075*Period[1] + .54);
       jQ = (.0962*Q1 + .5769*Q1[2] - .5769*Q1[4] -
       .0962*Q1[6])*(.075*Period[1] + .54);
                                          (continued)
```

Figure 17.1.   MAMA EasyLanguage code.

```
{Phasor addition for 3 bar averaging)}
I2 = I1 - jQ;
Q2 = Q1 + jI;

{Smooth the I and Q components before applying
  the discriminator}
I2 = .2*I2 + .8*I2[1];
Q2 = .2*Q2 + .8*Q2[1];

{Homodyne Discriminator}
Re = I2*I2[1] + Q2*Q2[1];
Im = I2*Q2[1] - Q2*I2[1];
Re = .2*Re + .8*Re[1];
Im = .2*Im + .8*Im[1];
If Im <> 0 and Re <> 0 then Period =
  360/ArcTangent(Im/Re);
If Period > 1.5*Period[1] then Period =
  1.5*Period[1];
If Period < .67*Period[1] then Period =
  .67*Period[1];
If Period < 6 then Period = 6;
If Period > 50 then Period = 50;
Period = .2*Period + .8*Period[1];
SmoothPeriod = .33*Period + .67*SmoothPeriod[1];
If I1 <> 0 then Phase = (ArcTangent(Q1 / I1));
DeltaPhase = Phase[1] - Phase;
If DeltaPhase < 1 then DeltaPhase = 1;
alpha = Speed / DeltaPhase;
If alpha < SlowLimit then alpha = SlowLimit;
MAMA = alpha*Price + (1 - alpha)*MAMA[1];
FAMA = .5*alpha*MAMA + (1 - .5*alpha)*FAMA[1];

Plot1(MAMA, "MAMA");
Plot2(FAMA, "FAMA");

End;
```

Figure 17.1.   *(Continued).*

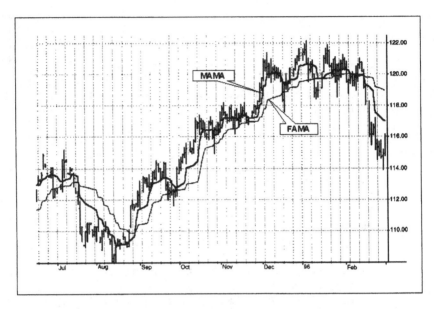

Figure 17.2.   MAMA rapidly ratchets to follow price.
Chart created with TradeStation2000i® by Omega Research, Inc.

The unique character of MAMA is shown in Figure 17.2. The thicker MAMA line ratchets closely behind the price. The thin FAMA line steps in time sequence with MAMA, but the movement is not as dramatic because its alpha is at half value. From Figure 17.2 it is clear that the two adaptive moving average lines only cross at major market reversals. Their action enables the creation of a trading system that is virtually free of whipsaw trades.

Key Points to Remember

- Most adaptive moving averages use momentum as the basis of the nonlinearity of alpha in an Exponential Moving Average (EMA).
- Mesa Adaptive Moving Average (MAMA) uses the Hilbert Transform phase rate of change to produce a ratcheting action of the adaptive moving average.
- MAMA is ideal as the basis of a trading system to minimize whipsaws.

Chapter 18

EHLERS FILTERS

To affinity—and beyond!

—Buzz Lightyear (paraphrased)

The most common filters used by traders are moving averages—either Simple Moving Averages (SMA) or Exponential Moving Averages (EMA). These are linear filters. Linear filters are optimal for smoothing stationary, slowly varying signals that are corrupted with high-frequency noise. Unfortunately, price data are not stationary much of the time. A coin flip experiment is an example of a statistical stationary process. However, if weighted coins are introduced into the experiment randomly, the statistics of the experiment now depend on which coin is used, and therefore are nonstationary. The signals we deal with can often be described statistically. For example, human speech has noiselike statistics. The process is nonstationary because it changes from moment to moment. Although speech has noiselike characteristics, that is not to say that it does not carry information. Price data resembles speech in statistical characteristics. The data are both noiselike and nonstationary. One of the main problems we encounter in trading when using technical analysis is that we must attempt to restore signals that are often nonstationary and are also corrupted by noise. When dealing with nonstationary signals that have sharp transitions of their mean or when dealing with impulsive noise, linear filtering techniques give poor results. In this chapter, I describe how to make some amazing nonlinear filters that better handle these signals.

The filters I have invented are nonlinear FIR filters. It turns out that they provide both extraordinary smoothing in sideways markets and aggressively follow major price movements with minimal lag. The development of my filters starts with a general class of FIR filters called Order Statistic (OS) filters. These filters are well-known for speech and image processing,[1] to sharpen edges, increase contrast, and for robust estimation. In contrast to linear filters, where temporal ordering of the samples is preserved, OS filters base their operation on the ranking of samples within the filter window. The data are ranked by their summary statistics, such as their mean or variance, rather than by their temporal position.

Among OS filters, the Median filter is the best known. In a Median filter, the output is the median value of all the data values within the observation window. As opposed to an averaging filter, the Median filter simply discards all data except the median value. In this way, impulsive noise spikes and extreme price data are eliminated rather than included in the average. The median value can fall at the first sample in the data window, at the last sample, or anywhere in between. Thus, temporal characteristics are lost. The Median filter tends to smooth out short-term variations that lead to whipsaw trades with linear filters. However, the lag of a Median filter in response to a sharp and sustained price movement is substantial—it necessarily is about half the filter window width. The response of a Median filter that has a 10-bar window width is shown in Figure 18.1. Note that the filter did not respond to small price movements in October/November or in January/February, which possibly could have eliminated several potential whipsaw trades that would have been produced by linear filters. Finding the median is a simple sorting problem, and, conveniently, TradeStation contains a median function. Therefore, I will not provide code for a Median filter. Median filters can be smoothed with an EMA to make them more presentable and easier to read.

---

[1]Pitas, Ioannis, and Anastasios N. Venetsanopoulos. "Order Statistics in Digital Image Processing," *Proceedings of the IEEE* 80/12 (1992): 1893–1921.

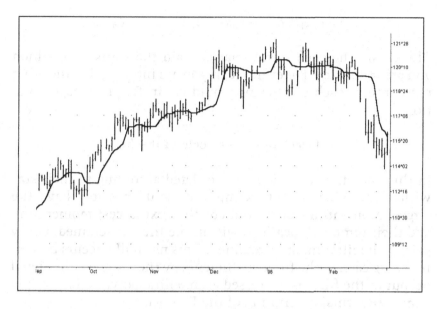

Figure 18.1. Response of a 10-bar Median filter.
Chart created with TradeStation2000i® by Omega Research, Inc.

Like OS filters, Ehlers filters are robust. Additionally, they exploit both the rank-order and temporal characteristics of the data. That is, the Ehlers filter maintains the temporal affinity between its coefficients and the statistic in use. The generalized Ehlers filter can be oriented to any statistic of your choice, making it extremely easy to calculate. The most obvious statistic to use is price momentum because these data enable the nonlinear Ehlers filter to rapidly follow price changes (as they enable the KAMA IIR filter to do the same). The range of statistic used is virtually limitless. For example, the Ehlers filter could be nonlinear with respect to acceleration (the rate change of momentum), Signal-to-Noise Ratio, volume, money flow (delta price times volume), and so on. Even other indicators, such as Stochastic or Relative Strength Indicators (RSIs) can be used as a statistic. This will become more apparent after we explain the calculating procedure.

The Ehlers filter has a formulation similar to that of the FIR filter. If y is the filter output and x_i is the ith input across a filter window width n, then the equation is

$$y = c_1 x_1 + c_2 x_2 + c_3 x_3 + c_4 x_4 + \ldots + c_n x_n$$

The c's are the coefficients that contain the statistic in which you are interested. For example, if you are interested in the 5-bar momentum, each coefficient would be, in EasyLanguage notation,

$$\text{Price[count]} - \text{Price[count} + 5]$$

In this way, the coefficients are ordered according to their size within the window. For example, c_3 could possibly have the largest momentum and c_1 could be the next largest momentum, and their temporal locations within the filter is retained. Unity gain of the filter must be retained. This naturally occurs by normalizing each of the filter coefficients by their sum so the signal output of the filter is expressed as an affine polynomial. So, the complete formal description of the Ehlers filter is

$$y = \frac{\sum_{i=0}^{n-1} c_i x_i}{\sum_{i=0}^{n-1} c_i}$$

The statistic used in the Ehlers filters should be detrended for maximum effectiveness. If we do not detrend the statistic, each of the coefficients will have a large common term relative to any differences there may be between them. If the coefficients have a large common term, the Ehlers filter behaves almost identical to an SMA.

The EasyLanguage code for the Ehlers filter is given in Figure 18.2 for the particular example of a 5-bar momentum.

The example filter has 15 coefficients, although the array of coefficients is dimensioned to 25 to allow experimentation using a longer filter. (If a filter longer than 25 samples is desired, the dimension of the Array must be increased accordingly.) In the first calculation, we find each coefficient in the filter as the 5-bar momentum. The next computation sums the numerator

```
Inputs: Price((H+L)/2),
        Length(15);

Vars: count(0),
      SumCoef(0),
      Num(0),
      Filt(0);

Array: Coef[25](0);

{Coefficients can be computed using any statistic of
  choice --------- a 5 bar momentum is used as an
  example}

For count = 0 to Length - 1 begin
      Coef[count] = AbsValue(Price[count] -
        Price[Count + 5]);
end;

{Sum across the numerator and across all coefficients}
Num = 0;
SumCoef =0;
For count = 0 to Length -1 begin
      Num = Num + Coef[count]*Price[count];
      SumCoef = SumCoef + Coef[count];
end;
Filt = Num / SumCoef;

Plot1(Filt, "Ehlers");
```

Figure 18.2.   EasyLanguage code to compute Ehlers filters.

as the product of each coefficient and the price at the corresponding sample, and sums the coefficients alone. Finally, the filter is completed by taking the ratio of the numerator to the coefficient sum. The performance of this filter is shown in Figure 18.3.

Figure 18.3 illustrates how the momentum-derived Ehlers filter clearly responds quickly to rapid price movements while rejecting minor price movements to a greater degree. This kind

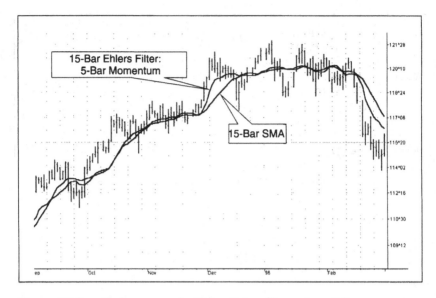

Figure 18.3.   Performance of a 15-bar Ehlers filter using a 5-bar momentum compared to the performance of a 15-bar SMA.
Chart created with TradeStation2000i® by Omega Research, Inc.

of filter can be used to quickly respond to changes in trend direction without producing the whipsaws that are so prevalent when linear filters are employed. The Ehlers filter can be rendered very aggressive by squaring each coefficient.

The greater flexibility of Ehlers filters opens up whole new avenues of technical analysis research. For example, the statistic can be some tangible parameter of market activity such as money flow or volume. Also, more arcane parameters such as Signal-to-Noise Ratio can be used. In this case, the coefficients where the Signal-to-Noise Ratio is the greatest would have the largest weight, discounting the price data values where the Signal-to-Noise Ratio is less. Also, Ehlers filters can be adaptive. For example, the length of the 5-bar momentum Ehlers filter in our example could be adaptive to the length of the measured cycle period. Such a filter would be both adaptive and nonlinear.

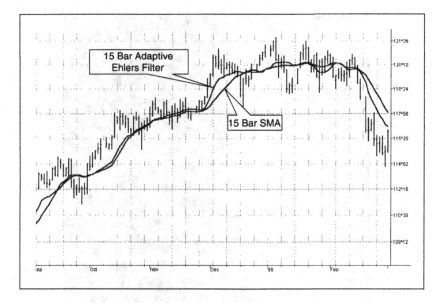

Figure 18.4. Performance of an adaptive 15-bar Ehlers filter compared to the performance of a 15-bar SMA.
Chart created with TradeStation2000i® by Omega Research, Inc.

The flexibility and adaptability of the Ehlers filter is demonstrated in Figure 18.4, where the statistic used is the difference between the current price and the previously calculated value of the filter.

Since whipsaw signals tend to be suppressed with Ehlers filters, exciting new oscillators can be created by taking the difference of Ehlers filters that have different scales. Imagine indicators analogous to RSI or Stochastics without whipsaws! Oscillators could also be generated from the differences of Ehlers filters by using a different statistic in each filter.

Regardless of the flexibility of the Ehlers filter, it is useful to step back and reflect on the motivation for deriving this filter type. By so doing, we may discover an optimum solution for the calculation of the coefficients. We know market data are most often nonstationary. We also know that we want to follow the sharp and sustained movements of price as closely as possible. This led us to use the Median filter as an edge detector. But not

Figure 18.5.   Visualizing the sharpness of an edge.

all edges are the same. We can visualize the sharpness of edges in Figure 18.5 by imagining looking down on this figure as we would on a piece of paper, illuminated from above our left shoulder, and hanging over the edge of a desk. The edge at the top of Figure 18.5 is very sharp, as if the paper were creased. Continuing down Figure 18.5, the light diffusion is more dispersed, giving the illusion that the edge becomes more rounded. In fact, the shading of Figure 18.5 was generated by a Gaussian function whose standard deviation increased from top to bottom.

If we consider the gray shading levels in Figure 18.5 as distances, we have a way of computing filter coefficients in terms of sharpness of the edge. White is the maximum distance in one direction from the median gray, and black is the maximum distance in the other direction. In this sense, distance is a measure of departure from the edge, taking into account the edge sharpness. Transitioning to price charts, the difference in prices can be imagined as a distance. Recalling the Pythagorean Theorem (in which the length of the hypotenuse of a triangle is equal to the sum of the squares of the lengths of the other two sides), we can apply it to our needs and say that a generalized length at any data sample is the square root of the sum of the squares of the price difference between that price and each of the prices back for the length of the filter window. The distances squared at each data point are the coefficients of the Ehlers filter. The calculation of the distancelike coefficients is perhaps best understood with reference to the EasyLanguage code for the filter in Figure 18.6. If

```
Inputs: Price((H+L)/2),
        Length(15);

Vars: count(0),
      LookBack(0),
      SumCoef(0),
      Num(0),
      Filt(0);

Array: Coef[25](0),
       Distance2[25](0);

For count = 0 to Length - 1 begin
     Distance2[count] = 0;
     For LookBack = 1 to Length - 1 begin
          Distance2[count] = Distance2[count] +
            (Price[count] - Price[count + LookBack])*
            (Price[count] - Price[count + LookBack]);
     end;
     Coef[count] = Distance2[count];
end;
Num = 0;
SumCoef =0;
For count = 0 to Length -1 begin
     Num = Num + Coef[count]*Price[count];
     SumCoef = SumCoef + Coef[count];
end;
If SumCoef <> 0 then Filt = Num / SumCoef;

Plot1(Filt, "Ehlers");
```

Figure 18.6. EasyLanguage code for the distance coefficient Ehlers filter.

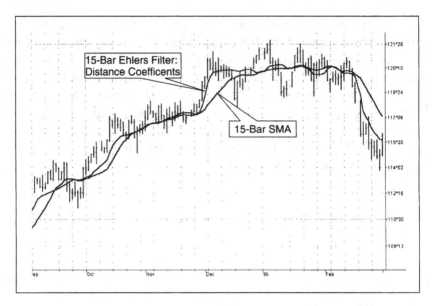

Figure 18.7   Performance of the distance coefficient Ehlers filter.
Chart created with TradeStation2000i® by Omega Research, Inc.

the prices across the filter observation window are the same, then the coefficients of the filter are all the same, and we have the equivalent of an SMA. However, if the prices shift rapidly, the distances from the increased price points increase, and higher weights are given to these filter coefficients. The performance of the distance coefficient Ehlers filter is shown in Figure 18.7.

The filter coefficients can be made to be even more nonlinear than calculated in Figure 18.6. For example, the distance can be cubed or raised to the fourth power (by squaring the squared distance). A reciprocal Gaussian response is an even more nonlinear function of distance that we can use to calculate the filter coefficients. These more nonlinear responses follow the edges in price movement more aggressively. However, the very fact that they are so nonlinear removes much of the gray area in the response. The most nonlinear calculations produce results that are not discernable from median filters. The coefficients become black and white. The focus of our current research is to identify the onset of the price shift more accurately. The currently calculated distance functions are related to the change of price. In calculus terms, this is the first derivative. The shift of the rate change of price is the ideal identifier for the impending price move. In calculus terms, we can use the maximum of the second derivative to pinpoint the onset of the price change. The challenge is how to translate the second derivative into filter coefficients without introducing so much noise that the filter response is unusable.

The opportunities to use Ehlers filters in technical analysis are limitless. I am sure whole books will be devoted to cataloging the various statistics and applications where they work best. In the meantime, you will have the opportunity to exploit them for your own fun and profit.

Key Points to Remember

- Market data tend to be nonstationary much of the time. Therefore, adaptive technique or nonlinear data processing is required for maximum effectiveness.
- Ehlers filters are easy to compute. Compute the coefficient at each position in the filter for the chosen statistic. Compute the filter as the sum of the product of the prices times the coefficients divided by the sum of coefficients.
- Ehlers filters aggressively follow sustained price shifts and revert to a FIR filter response when the prices are in a trading range.
- A host of indicators and trading systems can be derived from Ehlers filters.

Chapter 19

MEASURING MARKET SPECTRA

Science is the refusal to believe
on the basis of hope.

—C.P. Snow

All major trading software platforms have the Fast Fourier Transform (FFT) tool available. Yet, using FFTs for market analysis is analogous to using a chainsaw at a wood-carving convention. While chainsaws are certainly effective, they are not the correct tool for the job. Back in 1986, I wrote one of the first FFTs for traders using BASIC code for an Apple II computer.[1] Although FFTs are powerful tools for many applications, there are better and more precise tools we can use for market analysis.

A problem with FFTs is that they are subject to several constraints. One constraint is that there can only be an integer number of cycles in the data window. For example, if we have 64 data samples in our measurement window (a 64-point FFT), the longest cycle length we can measure is 64 bars. The next longest length has 2 cycles in the window, or $^{64}/_2 = 32$-bar cycle. The next longest lengths are $^{64}/_3 = 21.3$ bars, $^{64}/_4 = 16$ bars, and so on. Therefore, the integer constraint results in a lack of resolution. In other words, a large gap exists between the measured cycle lengths that can be produced, in the length of cycle periods in which we wish to work. We cannot tell if the real cycle is 14 bars

---

[1]Kaufman, Perry J. *Trading Systems and Methods*. 3rd ed. New York: John Wiley & Sons, 1998.

197

or 19 bars in length. Therefore, the spectrum measurement necessarily has a low resolution.

The only way to increase the FFT resolution is to increase the length of the data window. If we increase the data length to 256 samples, we reach a 1-bar resolution for cycle lengths in the vicinity of a 16-bar cycle. However, obtaining this resolution highlights another constraint. The cycle measurement is valid only if the data are stationary over the entire data window. This means that a 16-bar cycle must have the same amplitude and phase over the total 16 full cycles. In other words, using daily data, a 16-day cycle must be consistently present for over a full year for the measurement to be valid. Can this happen? I don't think so! By the time a 16-bar cycle occurs for more than several cycles, it will be observed by every trader in the world and they will destroy that cycle by jumping all over it. Its potential long-term existence is the very cause of its demise! The only way to obtain a valid high-resolution cycle measurement is to select a technique for which only a short amount of data is required. MESA fills this requirement.

Still not convinced? Let us demonstrate this point with some measurements. Figure 19.1 shows how we have converted the amplitude of a conventional bell-shaped spectrum display into gray density according to the amplitude of the spectral components. Think of the gray shading ranging from white hot to ice cold. Shading the amplitude enables us to plot the spectrum contour below the price bars in time synchronization. A white line represents a sharp, well-defined cycle. A wide light gray splotch tells us that the top of the bell-shaped curve is very broad and that the measurement has poor resolution. Figure 19.2 is a 64-point FFT measurement of a theoretical 24-bar sine wave. Since this is a theoretical cycle with no noise, the measurement should be precise. But it is not! The spectral contour shows that the measurement has very poor resolution. The measured length could as easily be 15 bars as 30 bars. Figure 19.3 is a 64-point FFT taken on real market data. Here, we can barely determine that the cycle is moving, but cannot definitively identify it. Revisiting these data later using the MESA measurement technique, we will see just how much more precise the MESA system is.

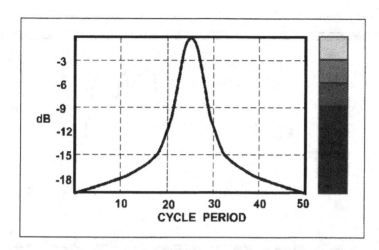

Figure 19.1.   Spectrum amplitude to shading conversion.

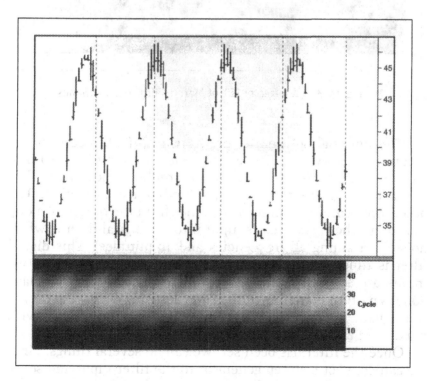

Figure 19.2.   A 64-point FFT of a theoretical 24-bar cycle.

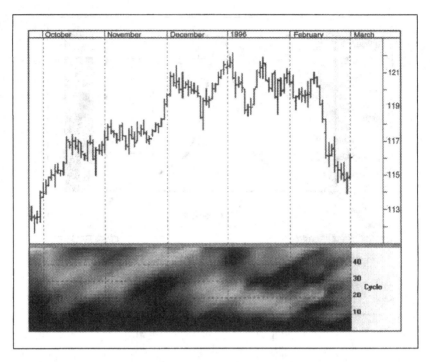

Figure 19.3.   A 64-point FFT of March 1996 Treasury Bonds.

The notional schematic for the way MESA measures the spectrum is shown in Figure 19.4. The data sample is fed into one input of a comparator. This data sample can be any length— it can even be less than a single dominant cycle period. The other input into the comparator comes from the output of a digital filter. The signal that is input into the digital filter is white noise (containing all frequencies and amplitudes). This digital filter is tuned by the output of the comparator until the two inputs are as nearly alike as possible. In short, what we have done is pattern matching in the time domain. We have removed the signal components with the filter, leaving the residual with maximum entropy (maximum disarray).

Once the filter has been set, we can do several things. First, we can connect a sweep generator to the filter input and sense the relative amplitude of the output as the frequency band is swept. This produces the bell-shaped spectral estimate similar

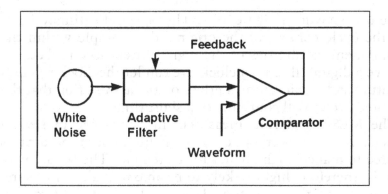

Figure 19.4.   How MESA measures the spectrum.

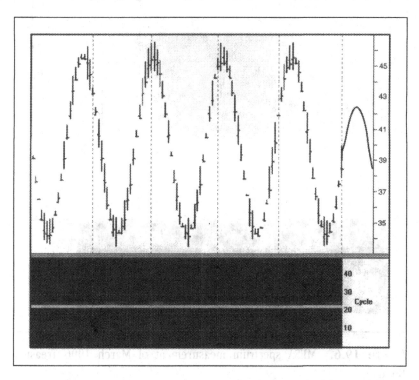

Figure 19.5.   MESA measurement of a theoretical 24-bar cycle.

to the one shown in Figure 19.1. This spectral estimate is, in fact, the cycle content of the original data sample within the measurement capabilities of the digital filter. Second, because we have a digital filter on a clock, we can let the clock run into the future and predict futures prices on the assumption that the measured cycles will continue for a short time.

The MESA spectrum measurement is notable in several respects. Most important, only a small amount of data is required to make a high-quality measurement. The MESA algorithm is, therefore, highly likely to be able to make a measurement using nearly stationary data, as the data need remain stationary for only a short while. As previously indicated, cycle

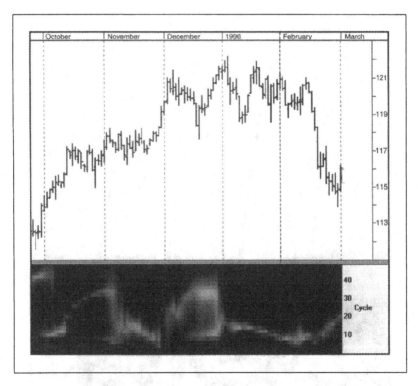

Figure 19.6. MESA spectrum measurement of March 1996 Treasury Bonds.

measurements are valid only if the data are stationary. Also, because the MESA algorithm requires only a short amount of data, we are able to exploit the short-term coherency of the market. This is entirely consistent with the Telegrapher's Equation solution to the Drunkard's Walk problem. This means that when the market is in a Cycle Mode, the measured cycle has predictive capability. Additionally, the MESA approach makes high-resolution spectral estimates. The high-quality measurement of the theoretical 24-bar cycle is shown in Figure 19.5, where only one cycle's worth of data is used in the measurements. Here, the spectral contour is a single line, meaning that the bell-shaped curve is just a spike centered at the 24-bar cycle period. Figure 19.6 shows the ebb and flow of the measured cycle for the March 1996 Treasury Bonds. While clearly illustrated with the MESA approach, this cycle characteristic was only inferred in the FFT measurement.

Key Points to Remember

- The Fast Fourier Transform (FFT) is not the proper tool to analyze market data.
- An FFT can measure only an integer number of cycles within its observation window.
- An FFT requires a large amount of data to achieve high-resolution measurements. If we are looking at market data over a long time span, the FFT is useless because the data cannot fulfill the requirement to remain relatively stationary in order to achieve a valid measurement.
- MESA operates by pattern matching in the time domain. Data outside the short observation window are rejected.
- There is typically only one dominant cycle in the market at a time.

Chapter 20

OPTIMUM PREDICTIVE FILTERS

The impossible is often the untried.

—JIM GOODWIN

Technical analysis is necessarily reactive to the action of the market. The indicators we develop are largely generated to sense the direction in which the price is expected to go. The predictive nature of these indicators is based on correlation to past experience, so the expectation logic runs as follows: If something happened before, it will very likely happen again. However, no indicator is truly predictive in the scientific sense.

In this chapter, I describe a predictive filter, explain how to generate this filter, and (most important) define the conditions under which the filter can be most effectively used. Like all technical indicators, the Optimum Predictive filter cannot be used universally. However, carefully observing those conditions where it is appropriate can make the Optimum Predictive filter a valuable addition to your arsenal of technical analysis weapons. I extrapolate from the concept of Optimum Predictive filters and discuss another way to eliminate lag from moving averages.

Optimum Predictive Filters

An Optimum Predictive filter is simply the difference between the original function and its Exponential Moving Average

(EMA).[1] That's it! It really is that simple! While the implementation is rather uncomplicated, the derivation is considerably more complex. In general, the response of an optimum system is described by the solution of the Wiener-Hopf equation, a discussion of which is well beyond the scope of this book.

Having defined an Optimum Predictive filter, we must quickly specify the conditions that are required for that filter to be valid. There are two such conditions. One condition is that the amplitude swings of the original function must be limited. The second condition is that the probability of the function passing through zero value must satisfy a Poisson probability distribution. It turns out that these conditions are easy to satisfy.

Without getting into the math, a Poisson probability distribution tells us that the number of crossings we expect are not far removed from the average number of crossings. This is simply another way of saying that the market must be in a Cycle Mode. An approximation to the Poisson probability distribution can be achieved using market data if the prices have been detrended. It is absolutely crucial that we detrend because buy/sell signals are obtained by the crossing of the signal and the predictive filter lines. If the price has not been properly detrended to meet the Poisson probability constraint, the lines will not cross correctly.

Since we desire a predictive filter, lag must be held to an absolute minimum. However, the price data must have at least some smoothing to separate the valid signals from the false. We use a 4-bar Weighted Moving Average (WMA) because it has a lag of only 1 bar. We detrend by taking the smoothed price less the smoothed price 2 bars ago. This particular momentum has the phase characteristics of a Hilbert Transformer and a lag of only 1 bar. As a practical matter, we need to smooth again after detrending to minimize the noise that was introduced by the detrending action. We therefore have 3 bars of lag just to obtain the proper detrended signal. This will cause some phase distortion of the output. The phase lag due to the 2-bar lag is $3*360/$

---

[1]Lee, Y.W. *Statistical Theory of Communication*. New York: John Wiley & Sons, 1966.

Period. However, the Hilbert Transformer provides a 90-degree phase lead. Therefore, if the data have a cycle period of 12 bars, the detrended price will be exactly in phase with the original price. The detrended price will lead in phase for longer cycle periods and will lag in phase for shorter cycle periods. When the market is in a Trend Mode, the cycle periods tend to be longer. As a result, under Trend Mode conditions, signals that are too early will be produced. However, the Poisson probability criterion is not likely to be met under these conditions. In any event, the signals are invalid when the market is in a Trend Mode. These limitations must be accepted.

The filtered output of the EMA should lag the detrended price by about 45 degrees in phase. When we see a 45-degree phase lag, we know that the dominant cycle component is approximately at the cutoff frequency of the EMA filter. The phasor diagram in Figure 20.1 shows us why this is so and demonstrates why the prediction works at all. The Detrender is a phasor at a reference angle of zero and rotates counterclockwise. The DetrendEMA lags the Detrender by about 45 degrees.

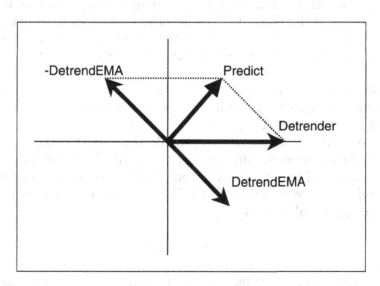

Figure 20.1. The predict Phasor Diagram.

When we subtract the latter from the former in vector arithmetic, we reverse the direction of the DetrendEMA and then perform vector addition. When we do this, the Predict vector results.

Since the DetrendEMA is at the cutoff frequency of the EMA, its amplitude is about 70 percent of the Detrender amplitude. At a 45-degree angle, the real and imaginary components are equal at a relative amplitude of 0.5 (0.7*Cos(45)). The vector subtraction in complex arithmetic is Predict = 1 − 0.5 + j0.5 = 0.5 + j0.5. Since the two components of the Predict phasor are both 0.5, the absolute amplitude of the Predict phasor is 0.7 from the Pythagorean Theorem. Therefore, the Predict phasor must be multiplied by 1.4 to have the same normalized amplitude as the Detrender phasor.

Frequency components within the EMA passband will not be attenuated as much as those components outside the passband. Additionally, the EMA passband's frequency components will have less than 45 degrees of phase lag. If the phase lag is small, then the vector difference between the Detrender and the DetrendEMA will be a vector with a very small amplitude. The small-amplitude Predict vector contributes little as a predictor. However, if the DetrendEMA lags the Detrender by much more than 45 degrees, it falls outside the passband of the EMA filter, thus severely reducing its amplitude. In this case, the Predict vector will lead the Detrender by less than 45 degrees and will also have a very small amplitude. Therefore, having the frequency component outside the EMA passband also does not contribute to an effective predictor.

A solution does exist to provide the proper phase relationship. First, we must compute the market cycle, using the Hilbert Transform. Then, we use the computed cycle period to compute the desired alpha for the EMA. From Chapter 13, we remember that the calculation is

$$\alpha = 1 - e^{-2\pi/P_o}$$

Figure 20.2 gives us the code to perform all the calculations for the Optimum Predictor. As we have seen before, the major-

```
Inputs:      Price((H+L)/2);

Vars: Smooth(0),
      Detrender(0),
      I1(0),
      Q1(0),
      jI(0),
      jQ(0),
      I2(0),
      Q2(0),
      Re(0),
      Im(0),
      Period(0),
      SmoothPeriod(0),
      Detrender2(0),
      Smooth2(0),
      alpha(0),
      DetrendEMA(0),
      Predict(0);

If CurrentBar > 5 then begin
      Smooth = (4*Price + 3*Price[1] + 2*Price[2] +
          Price[3]) / 10;
      Detrender = (.0962*Smooth + .5769*Smooth[2] -
          .5769*Smooth[4] - .0962*Smooth[6])*(.075*
          Period[1] + .55);

      {Compute InPhase and Quadrature components}
      Q1 = (.0962*Detrender + .5769*Detrender[2] -
          .5769*Detrender[4] - .0962*Detrender[6])*
          (.075*Period[1] + .55);
      I1 = Detrender[3];

      {Advance the phase of I1 and Q1 by 90 degrees}
      jI = (.0962*I1 + .5769*I1[2] - .5769*I1[4] -
          .0962*I1[6])*(.075*Period[1] + .55);
      jQ = (.0962*Q1 + .5769*Q1[2] - .5769*Q1[4] -
          .0962*Q1[6])*(.075*Period[1] + .55);

      {Phasor addition for 3 bar averaging)}
      I2 = I1 - jQ;
      Q2 = Q1 + jI;
                                         (continued)
```

Figure 20.2. EasyLanguage code for the Optimum Predictor.

```
{Smooth the I and Q components before applying
    the discriminator}
I2 = .2*I2 + .8*I2[1];
Q2 = .2*Q2 + .8*Q2[1];

{Homodyne Discriminator}
Re = I2*I2[1] + Q2*Q2[1];
Im = I2*Q2[1] - Q2*I2[1];
Re = .2*Re + .8*Re[1];
Im = .2*Im + .8*Im[1];
If Im <> 0 and Re <> 0 then Period =
    360/ArcTangent(Im/Re);
If Period > 1.5*Period[1] then Period =
    1.5*Period[1];
If Period < .67*Period[1] then Period =
    .67*Period[1];
If Period < 6 then Period = 6;
If Period > 50 then Period = 50;
Period = .2*Period + .8*Period[1];
SmoothPeriod = .33*Period + .67*SmoothPeriod[1];

{Optimum Predictor}
Detrender2 = .5*Smooth - .5*Smooth[2];
Smooth2 = (4*Detrender2 + 3*Detrender2[1] +
    2*Detrender2[2] + Detrender2[3]) / 10;
alpha = 1 - ExpValue(-6.28/Period);
DetrendEMA = alpha*Smooth2 +
    (1 - alpha)*DetrendEMA[1];
Predict = 1.4*(Smooth2 - DetrendEMA);

Plot1(Smooth2, "Signal");
Plot2(Predict, "Predict");

End;
```

Figure 20.2.   *(Continued).*

ity of the code involves the computation of the period using the Homodyne Discriminator algorithm. Once the period has been computed, the Optimum Predictor is found in just a few lines of code. First, the minimum-length Hilbert Transformer is used to compute the Detrender2 value from the prices that have been smoothed by the 4-bar Weighted Moving Average (WMA). Detrender2 is smoothed in the 4-bar WMA to produce Smooth2. The alpha of the EMA is computed from the computed period, and the EMA of Smooth2 is taken using that alpha and is called the DetrendEMA. The difference between Smooth2 and the DetrendEMA is multiplied by 1.4 to produce the Predict phasor. Finally, the Smooth2 and Predict phasors are plotted as indicators.

The Optimum Predictor is plotted in Figure 20.3 as the subgraph below the price chart. Buy and sell signals occur when the Predict and Smooth2 lines cross. Most of these signals are indeed prescient. The Optimum Predictor could probably work best in trading systems when used in conjunction with other rules to eliminate the false signals. Alternatively, the turning point of the LeadSine of the Sine wave Indicator could be used as a confirming signal.

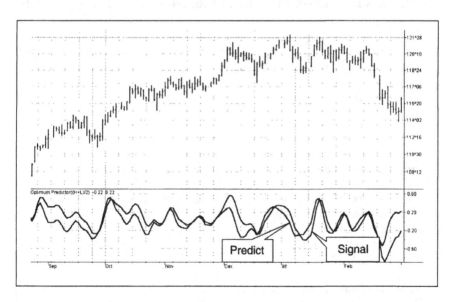

Figure 20.3. The Optimum Predictor accurately indicates many price turning points.

Chart created with TradeStation 2000i® by Omega Research, Inc.

Predictive Moving Averages

The concept of taking a difference of lagging line from the original function to produce a leading function suggests extending the concept to moving averages. There is no direct theory for this, but it seems to work pretty well. If I take a 7-bar WMA of prices, that average lags the prices by 2 bars. If I take a 7-bar WMA of the first average, this second average is delayed another 2 bars. If I take the difference between the two averages and add that difference to the first average, the result should be a smoothed line of the original price function with no lag. Sure, I could try to use more lag for the second moving average, which should produce a better predictive curve. However, remember the lesson of Chapter 3? An analysis curve cannot precede an event. You cannot predict an event before it occurs.

If we then take a 4-bar WMA of the smoothed line to create a 1-bar lag, this lagging line becomes a signal when the lines cross. This is as close to an ideal indicator as we can get. There

```
Inputs:        Price((H+L)/2);

Vars: WMA1(0),
      WMA2(0),
      Predict(0),
      Trigger(0);

WMA1 = (7*Price + 6*Price[1] + 5*Price[2] + 4*Price[3]
      + 3*Price[4] + 2*Price[5] + Price[6]) / 28;
WMA2 = (7*WMA1 + 6*WMA1[1] + 5*WMA1[2] + 4*WMA1[3] +
      3*WMA1[4] + 2*WMA1[5] + WMA1[6]) / 28;
Predict = 2*WMA1 - WMA2;
Trigger = (4*Predict + 3*Predict[1] + 2*Predict[2] +
Predict) / 10;

Plot1(Trigger, "Trigger");
Plot2(Predict, "Predict");
```

Figure 20.4.   EasyLanguage code to compute predictive averages.

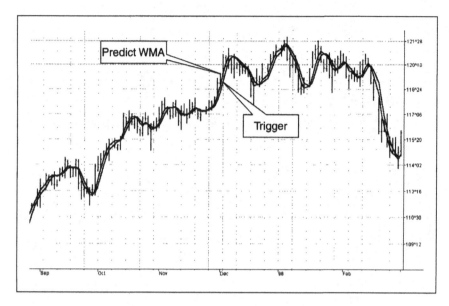

Figure 20.5. Predictive moving average and trigger signal.
Chart created with TradeStation 2000i® by Omega Research, Inc.

is no phase distortion. The code to compute this indicator is given in Figure 20.4. The code could hardly be simpler. A sample of the indicator is shown in Figure 20.5.

Key Points to Remember

- A theoretically optimum predictor exists.
- The Optimum Predictor is calculated as the difference between a detrended signal and its Exponential Moving Average (EMA).
- The EMA constant of the Optimum Predictor is computed using the measured dominant cycle as the cutoff period of the filter.
- Moving average lag can be eliminated by taking the moving average of the first moving average, taking the difference between them, and adding that difference back onto the first moving average.

Chapter 21

WHAT YOU SEE
IS WHAT YOU GET

Success is a journey, not a destination.

—BEN SWEETLAND

That famous half-glass of water—optimists see it as half-full and
pessimists see it as half-empty. An engineer sees the glass as having been designed with too much capacity. That which we see is
really a matter of perception. Market technicians have designed a
wide variety of techniques to visualize what has happened in the
past in order to infer what the future holds. Candlestick charts
and Point and Figure charts are two examples of charting price
data. When it comes to indicators, there is a plethora of wiggles,
squiggles, zigzags, channels, and so on, that requires volumes to
describe.

I would now like to add to this cacophony of displays one so
new and novel, one so sensitive, that it dramatically pinpoints
variations and anomalies that cannot be removed with mathematical filters—at least within the lag constraints imposed by
trading considerations. All we do is plot the InPhase and Quadrature components of the Hilbert Transform. We can certainly
plot these components in a subgraph below the price chart so
they resemble an oscillator. However, if we were to plot these
two components against each other in an orthogonal set of coordinates (an x-y plot), we would be exactly tracing out the phasor
diagram. Plotting the phasor is the objective of this process.

215

The first step in generating the phasor display is to compute the InPhase and Quadrature components exactly the way we did in Chapter 7. The only difference is that we must plot the I1 and Q1 components in a subgraph. Additionally, we must include a line of code to output the I1 and Q1 values into an ASCII file. Figure 21.1 leads you through this EasyLanguage code.

```
Inputs:     Price ((H+L)/2);

Vars: Smooth(0),
      Detrender(0),
      I1(0),
      Q1(0),
      jI(0),
      jQ(0),
      I2(0),
      Q2(0),
      Re(0),
      Im(0),
      Period(0),
      SmoothPeriod(0);

If CurrentBar > 5 then begin
    Smooth = (4*Price + 3*Price[1] + 2*Price[2] +
      Price[3]) / 10;
    Detrender = (.0962*Smooth + .5769*Smooth[2] -
      .5769*Smooth[4] - .0962*Smooth[6])*(.075*
      Period[1] + .54);

    {Compute InPhase and Quadrature components}
    Q1 = (.0962*Detrender + .5769*Detrender[2] -
      .5769*Detrender[4] - .0962*Detrender[6])*(.075*
      Period[1] + .54);
    I1 = Detrender[3];

    {Advance the phase of I1 and Q1 by 90 degrees}
                                        (continued)
```

Figure 21.1.   EasyLanguage code to create an ASCII file of InPhase and Quadrature data.

```
jI = (.0962*I1 + .5769*I1[2] - .5769*I1[4] -
  .0962*I1[6])*(.075*Period[1] + .55);
jQ = (.0962*Q1 + .5769*Q1[2] - .5769*Q1[4] -
  .0962*Q1[6])*(.075*Period[1] + .55);

{Phasor addition for 3 bar averaging)}
I2 = I1 - jQ;
Q2 = Q1 + jI;

{Smooth the I and Q components before applying
  the discriminator}
I2 = .2*I2 + .8*I2[1];
Q2 = .2*Q2 + .8*Q2[1];

{Homodyne Discriminator}
Re = I2*I2[1] + Q2*Q2[1];
Im = I2*Q2[1] - Q2*I2[1];
Re = .2*Re + .8*Re[1];
Im = .2*Im + .8*Im[1];
If Im <> 0 and Re <> 0 then Period =
  360/ArcTangent(Im/Re);
If Period > 1.5*Period[1] then Period =
  1.5*Period[1];
If Period < .67*Period[1] then Period =
  .67*Period[1];
If Period < 6 then Period = 6;
If Period > 50 then Period = 50;
Period = .2*Period + .8*Period[1];
SmoothPeriod = .33*Period + .67*SmoothPeriod[1];

Plot1(I1, "I");
Plot2(Q1, "Q");

If Date > Date[1] then Print(File("c:\hilbert\
  IQ.csv"), date, "," , I1, ",", Q1);

End;
```

Figure 21.1. *(Continued)*.

The final line of code creates a file in the HILBERT directory on your C: drive. You should have created this directory using Windows Explorer before you run the program. The file is IQ.CSV, a comma-delimited ASCII file. You will import this file into Excel to generate the phasor display. Reading the file into Excel is straightforward. Just click FILE . . . OPEN and position C:\HILBERT in the Look In dialog box. Change the Files of Type dialog box to Text Files. The file IQ should then appear in the main dialog box. Highlight this file and click OPEN, and the three columns of the file will be displayed.

The phasor is created by highlighting roughly 30 rows of the two right-hand columns and clicking on the Chart Wizard in the Excel toolbar. In the first step of the Wizard, select the XY(Scatter) Plot and then choose the option to show the data points connected by smooth lines. Then click NEXT. Accept the defaults of the Wizard step 2 by clicking NEXT. In the Wizard step 3, select the Gridlines tab and then unselect the option to show major gridlines. Skip the Wizard step 4 by clicking FINISH. Click on the Series 1 legend and press the delete key to remove it. Finally, click on the chart and drag it so the gray graphical area is approximately square.

When you finish these operations, you will see a display similar to that shown in Figure 21.2, which depicts 29 points of a theoretical 30-bar sine wave. Due to the sign convention of computing the Quadrature component, the phasor track rotates clockwise. The cycle period can be estimated by counting the points in any quadrant and multiplying by 4. A perfect cycle will plot out as a circle in this kind of display.

We will now follow the phasor display over 120 trading days of the June 1996 Treasury Bonds contract. I like to use this old data set because it transitions from a Trend Mode to a Cycle Mode, and back to a Trend Mode. Since there are no intermediate modes, this data set facilitates explanation.

Figure 21.4 is a phasor plot for the data in the shaded box of Figure 21.3. Prices start in a Trend Mode at the left edge of the box. The starting point is located in the first quadrant of Figure 21.4. Since the market is in a Trend Mode, the phase hardly advances for about the first 17 bars. Then, due to the price dip

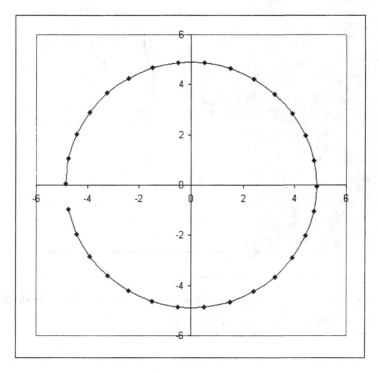

Figure 21.2   Twenty-nine points of a 30-bar sine wave. A perfect cycle plots as a circle in the phasor display.

and recovery, an apparent 12-bar cycle started. I arrived at this cycle period by counting the points in the left-half plane and doubling them. After another few points, this cycle fails and the Trend Mode is reestablished for data to the end of the shaded box. The data set ends in the Trend Mode in the fourth quadrant of the phasor plot.

The Trend Mode continues as depicted in the shaded box in Figure 21.5 and as a phasor in Figure 21.6, starting in the fourth quadrant. There is no definitive cycle movement in the first 22 bars except for about a half cycle of a 14-bar cycle. I estimated the period of this half cycle by counting the number of points in the right half of the plot for this point in time. After this brief cyclic burst, the phasor wanders almost aimlessly for another 15

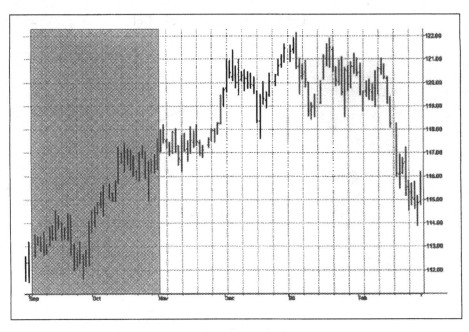

Figure 21.3. First 40-bar analysis section of Treasury Bonds. The shaded window is plotted as a phasor in Figure 21.4.
Chart created with TradeStation2000i® by Omega Research, Inc.

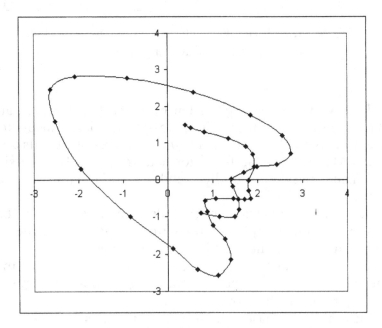

Figure 21.4. Phasor diagram for Figure 21.3 data.

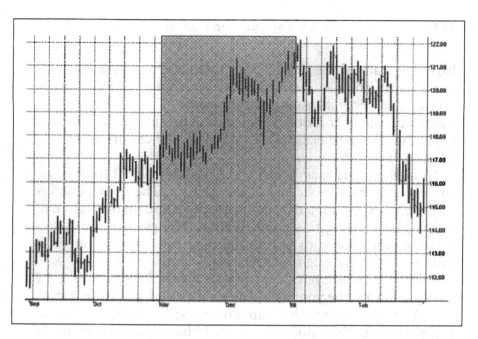

Figure 21.5. Second 40-bar analysis section of Treasury Bonds. The shaded window is plotted as a phasor in Figure 21.6.

Chart created with TradeStation2000i® by Omega Research, Inc.

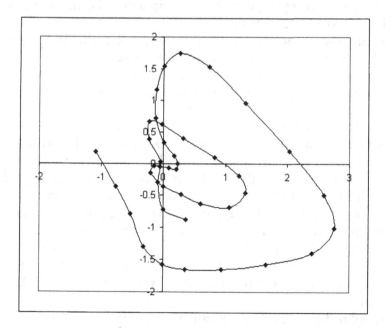

Figure 21.6. Phasor diagram for Figure 21.5 data.

bars. The path of the phasor even turns counterclockwise during this period. A counterclockwise rotation theoretically means that time is running backwards. This is impossible. Therefore, the only rational explanation for the path of the phasor is that the market is in a Trend Mode, where the advancing of phase has no meaning.

A new cycle is established at the top of Figure 21.6, and continues for 14 bars to the end of the data set. The cycle period is about 20 bars, estimated by counting the points in the right half of the plane during this point in time. The cycle shape is certainly distorted due to large amplitude fluctuations, but it is rotating about the origin at a relatively constant rate.

Near textbook cycles continue in Figure 21.8 for about 1.5 cycles from the beginning of the data period shown in Figure 21.7. Just by counting the points over one full rotation, we can estimate the cycle period to be about 16 bars. However, about 21 bars from the beginning of the data set, another anomaly appears. Two very fast whiffles, or curlycues, appear in the data. The shorter of these appears to be about a 5-bar cycle superimposed on a 12-bar cycle; both of these appear to be superimposed on the preexisting 16-bar cycle.

Returning to the phasor diagram schematic, this time in Figure 21.9, we can see an explanation for these whiffles.

A shorter subordinate cycle can be viewed as a phasor that rotates at the tip of the Dominant Cycle phasor, rotating at a rate faster than that of the Dominant Cycle. The Dominant Cycle phasor is rotating at its own rate. Thus, an evanescent five-day cycle produces a signature like the smaller whiffle in Figure 21.8. In fact, the shorter whiffle is superimposed on the longer 12-bar whiffle. The really interesting point is that the two whiffles indicate that the phase of the dominant cycle has stopped advancing, signaling the beginning of a Trend Mode. With this identification, we see that the Trend Mode started about 17 bars before the end of the data. Having identified the Trend onset well before the major price movement, we are well-equipped to maximize the profit of the Trend movement.

A subordinate cycle does not necessarily have to be a complete cycle. Fractional subordinate cycles can account for erratic

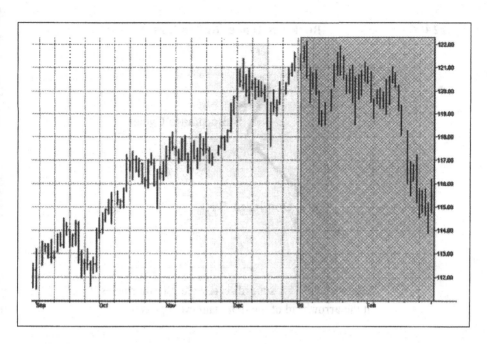

Figure 21.7 Third 40-bar analysis section of Treasury Bonds. The shaded window is plotted as a phasor in Figure 21.8.
Chart created with TradeStation2000i® by Omega Research, Inc.

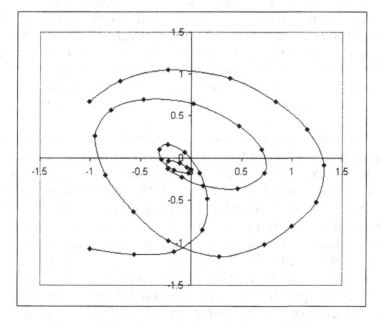

Figure 21.8. Phasor diagram for Figure 21.7 data.

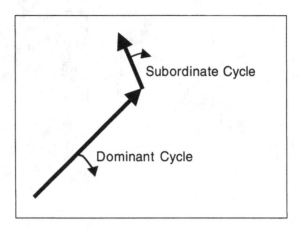

Figure 21.9. A subordinate cycle phasor rotates
at the arrowhead of the dominant cycle phasor.

paths in the phasor plot, such as the one that exists near the origin of Figure 21.6.

Subordinate cycles whose periods are longer than the period
of the dominant cycle are more difficult to visualize. They
throw the trajectory of the dominant cycle off center. Whether
the subordinate cycle is shorter or longer than the Dominant
Cycle, the phasor plot immediately identifies the impact of subordinate cycles without performing any additional filtering.
Additional filtering would certainly introduce lag that would
make further analysis even more difficult.

The key advantage of being acquainted with the phasor plot
is that you now have a tool to precisely estimate the cyclic turning points. You want to sell when the InPhase component is at
its maximum and buy when the InPhase component is at its
minimum. These buy and sell rules are subject, however, to the
lag of the computation of the InPhase component. Reviewing
the EasyLanguage code, we see that there is a 1-bar lag due to the
4-bar WMA, a 3-bar lag due to the detrending (the center of the
filter), and a 3-bar lag for the final computation of I1. The buying
and selling opportunity must account for this 7-bar lag in the
computation of the InPhase component. If you have a 14-bar

dominant cycle, the 7-bar lag constitutes a 180-degree shift of the phasor location (i.e., a half cycle). Keep in mind that the detrending operation in the computation introduced a 90-degree phase lead. Thus, you need compensate only for a net 90-degree lag (a quarter cycle) for this 14-bar cycle. Said another way, you must anticipate the maximum InPhase component by 3.5 bars (1¾ bars) for a selling opportunity and anticipate the minimum InPhase component by 3.5 bars for a buying opportunity. This precision technique is vastly superior to the half-cycle offsets you may have seen described in most trading literature.

Since the compensation calculation is so important, we will try to clarify by using another example. Suppose the dominant cycle is 21 days. The 7-bar lag would be one-third of a cycle, or 120 degrees. Removing the 90-degree lead that occurred due to detrending, the resultant lag of the InPhase component is only $120 - 90 = 30$ degrees. Thirty degrees is one-twelfth of a cycle, or 1.75 days in this example of a 21-bar cycle. So, in this case, you would have to anticipate the InPhase maxima and minima by only about two days.

Key Points to Remember

- A phasor diagram can be displayed by plotting the InPhase and Quadrature components of the Hilbert Transform in an Excel *x-y* scatter plot.
- The existence of more than one cycle can be identified by whiffles in the phasor diagram.
- The phasor diagram can help you anticipate the precise cyclic turning points in the market.

Chapter 22

MAKING STANDARD INDICATORS ADAPTIVE

When you've finished changing, you're finished.

—BENJAMIN FRANKLIN

It is not an uncommon occurrence that when I reach the end of a seminar, breathless and exhausted, I get a question like "Can I use the cycle to optimize an RSI?" My immediate unspoken reaction is "Why would someone want to do that?" I had just shown the audience the derivation of a theoretically optimum predictor, described the Sinewave Indicator that has few false whipsaw signals in the Trend Mode, and introduced an Instantaneous Trendline as a Trend Mode trading tool. After all, how can anything be better than theoretically optimum? Is there really a need for optimized conventional indicators? Then upon further reflection, I finally realized that this was exactly the question that intrigued me about technical analysis. I was unwilling to use a 14-day period in the RSI just because Welles Wilder said so. My quest for the best way to adapt to market conditions has led to all the research I have done, the results of which are chronicled in this book.

So, what is the best indicator? There is no single correct answer to that question. Everything is relative. Some indicators work better in one market than another. It may also depend on the preference of the trader. Using several indicators together may uncover a synergism unavailable to one indicator alone.

Many serviceable indicators exist. Improving them by making them adaptive to current market conditions should be the objective of every trader and is the object of this book. In this final chapter, I review three standard indicators: Relative Strength Indicator (RSI), Stochastic, and the Commodity Channel Indicator (CCI). This review includes a discussion of making these indicators adaptive to the measured cycle period using the Homodyne Discriminator.

RSI

Welles Wilder defined the RSI as[1]

$$RSI = 100 \ (100/(1 + RS))$$

where   RS = (Closes Up)/(Closes Down)
        = CU/CD

RS is shorthand for Relative Strength. That is, CU is the sum of the difference in closing prices over the observation period where that difference is positive. Similarly, CD is the sum of the difference in closing prices over the observation period where that difference is negative, but the sum is expressed as a positive number. When we substitute CU/CD for RS and simplify the RSI equation, we get

$$RSI = 100 - \frac{100}{1 + CU/CD}$$

$$= 100 - \frac{100CD}{CU + CD}$$

$$= \frac{100CU + 100CD - 100CD}{CU + CD}$$

$$RSI = \frac{100CU}{CU + CD}$$

---

[1]Wilder, J. Welles, Jr. *New Concepts in Technical Trading Systems.* Winston-Salem, NC: Hunter Publishing, 1978.

In other words, the RSI is the percentage of the sum of the delta closes up to the sum of all the delta closes over the observation period. The only variable here is the observation period. For maximum effectiveness, the observation period should be half the measured dominant cycle period. If the observation period is half the dominant cycle for a pure sine wave, the closes up is exactly equal to the total closes during part of the cycle from the valley to the peak. In this case, the RSI would have a value of 100. During another part of the cycle—the next half cycle—there would be no closes up. During this half cycle, the RSI would have a value of zero. So, in principle, half the measured cycle is the correct choice for the RSI observation period. In Figure 22.1, the EasyLanguage code measures the cycle period using the Homodyne Discriminator algorithm. It then uses that period as the basis for finding CU and CD, and computing the RSI. Since half the cycle period may not be the universal answer, we include a CycPart input as a modifier. This input allows you to optimize the observation period for each particular situation.

The optimized RSI tends to be in phase with the original price data. This suggests a way to turn a good indicator into a great indicator. If we subtract 50 from the optimized RSI, we would get a zero mean and thus tend to have Poisson-like statistics on the RSI's zero crossings. If that were the case, we could smooth the optimized RSI and make an Optimum Predictive filter from it. That way we could anticipate signals rather than wait for signals to cross the 30 percent and 70 percent marks for confirmation as is done with the standard indicator. I will leave it to you to decide which method best suits your needs and purposes.

Stochastic

The name of this indicator is rather amusing because the indicator has absolutely nothing to do with a statistical stochastic process. A stochastic process is defined as a randomly determined sequence of operations. When the indicator was forwarded by Rick Redmont to Tim Slater, then president of

```
Inputs:         Price((H+L)/2),
                CycPart(.5);

Vars: Smooth(0),
      Detrender(0),
      I1(0),
      Q1(0),
      jI(0),
      jQ(0),
      I2(0),
      Q2(0),
      Re(0),
      Im(0),
      Period(0),
      SmoothPeriod(0),
      count(0),
      CU(0),
      CD(0),
      RSI(0);

If CurrentBar > 5 then begin
    Smooth = (4*Price + 3*Price[1] + 2*Price[2] +
        Price[3]) / 10;
    Detrender = (.0962*Smooth + .5769*Smooth[2] -
        .5769*Smooth[4] - .0962*Smooth[6])*(.075*
        Period[1] + .54);

    {Compute InPhase and Quadrature components}
    Q1 = (.0962*Detrender + .5769*Detrender[2] -
        .5769*Detrender[4] - .0962*Detrender[6])*
        (.075*Period[1] + .54);
    I1 = Detrender[3];

    {Advance the phase of I1 and Q1 by 90 degrees}
    jI = (.0962*I1 + .5769*I1[2] - .5769*I1[4] -
        .0962*I1[6])*(.075*Period[1] + .54);
    jQ = (.0962*Q1 + .5769*Q1[2] - .5769*Q1[4] -
        .0962*Q1[6])*(.075*Period[1] + .54);
                                        (continued)
```

Figure 22.1.   EasyLanguage code to compute the adaptive RSI.

```
{Phasor addition for 3 bar averaging)}
I2 = I1 - jQ;
Q2 = Q1 + jI;

{Smooth the I and Q components before applying
  the discriminator}
I2 = .2*I2 + .8*I2[1];
Q2 = .2*Q2 + .8*Q2[1];

{Homodyne Discriminator}
Re = I2*I2[1] + Q2*Q2[1];
Im = I2*Q2[1] - Q2*I2[1];
Re = .2*Re + .8*Re[1];
Im = .2*Im + .8*Im[1];
If Im <> 0 and Re <> 0 then Period =
  360/ArcTangent(Im/Re);
If Period > 1.5*Period[1] then Period =
  1.5*Period[1];
If Period < .67*Period[1] then Period =
  .67*Period[1];
If Period < 6 then Period = 6;
If Period > 50 then Period = 50;
Period = .2*Period + .8*Period[1];
SmoothPeriod = .33*Period + .67*SmoothPeriod[1];

CU = 0;
CD = 0;
For count = 0 to Int(CycPart*SmoothPeriod) -
  1 begin
      If Close[count] - Close[count + 1] > 0 then
        CU = CU + (Close[count] -
        Close[count + 1]);
      If Close[count] - Close[count + 1] < 0 then
        CD = CD + (Close[count + 1] -
        Close[count]);
End;
If CU + CD <> 0 then RSI = 100*CU / (CU + CD);

Plot1(RSI, "RSI");

End;
```

Figure 22.1.　*(Continued).*

Compu-Trac, the word stochastic was scribbled in the margin. Tim thought that was a good name, and it stuck. The indicator has since been popularized by Dr. George Lane.

The Stochastic measures the current closing price relative to the lowest low over the observation period. It then normalizes this to the range between the highest high and the lowest low over the observation period. In equation form this is

$$\text{Stochastic} = \frac{\text{Close} - \text{LL}}{\text{HH} - \text{LL}}$$

If the current closing price is equal to the highest high over the observation period, then the Stochastic has a value of 1. If the current closing price is equal to the lowest low over the observation period, then the Stochastic has a value of zero. These are the limits over which the Stochastic can range.

To optimize the Stochastic for the measured cycle, the correct fraction of the cycle to use is one-half, as the Stochastic can range from its minimum to its maximum on each half cycle of the period. As before, the code for the optimized Stochastic (given in Figure 22.2) measures the cycle period using the Homodyne Discriminator algorithm and then uses that period as the basis for finding HH and LL and computing the Stochastic. Since half the cycle period may not be the universal answer, we include a CycPart input as a modifier. This input allows you to optimize the observation period for each particular situation.

The optimized Stochastic tends to be in phase with the original price data. This suggests a way to turn a good indicator into a great one. If we subtract 50 from the optimized Stochastic, we would get a zero mean and thus tend to have Poisson-like statistics on the Stochastic's zero crossings. If that were the case, we could smooth the optimized Stochastic and make an Optimum Predictive filter from it. That way we could anticipate signals rather than wait for signals to cross the 20 percent and 80 percent marks for confirmation as is done with the standard indicator. I will leave it to you to decide which method best suits your needs and purposes.

```
Inputs:        Price((H+L)/2),
               CycPart(.5);

Vars: Smooth(0),
      Detrender(0),
      I1(0),
      Q1(0),
      jI(0),
      jQ(0),
      I2(0),
      Q2(0),
      Re(0),
      Im(0),
      Period(0),
      SmoothPeriod(0),
      count(0),
      HH(0),
      LL(0),
      Stochastic(0);

If CurrentBar > 5 then begin
      Smooth = (4*Price + 3*Price[1] + 2*Price[2] +
        Price[3]) / 10;
      Detrender = (.0962*Smooth + .5769*Smooth[2] -
        .5769*Smooth[4] - .0962*Smooth[6])*
        (.075*Period[1] + .54);

      {Compute InPhase and Quadrature components}
      Q1 = (.0962*Detrender + .5769*Detrender[2] -
        .5769*Detrender[4] - .0962*Detrender[6])*
        (.075*Period[1] + .54);
      I1 = Detrender[3];

      {Advance the phase of I1 and Q1 by 90 degrees}
      jI = (.0962*I1 + .5769*I1[2] - .5769*I1[4] -
        .0962*I1[6])*(.075*Period[1] + .54);
      jQ = (.0962*Q1 + .5769*Q1[2] - .5769*Q1[4] -
        .0962*Q1[6])*(.075*Period[1] + .54);
                                          (continued)
```

Figure 22.2. EasyLanguage code to compute the adaptive Stochastic.

```
{Phasor addition for 3 bar averaging)}
I2 = I1 - jQ;
Q2 = Q1 + jI;

{Smooth the I and Q components before applying
  the discriminator}
I2 = .2*I2 + .8*I2[1];
Q2 = .2*Q2 + .8*Q2[1];

{Homodyne Discriminator}
Re = I2*I2[1] + Q2*Q2[1];
Im = I2*Q2[1] - Q2*I2[1];
Re = .2*Re + .8*Re[1];
Im = .2*Im + .8*Im[1];
If Im <> 0 and Re <> 0 then Period =
  360/ArcTangent(Im/Re);
If Period > 1.5*Period[1] then Period =
  1.5*Period[1];
If Period < .67*Period[1] then Period =
  .67*Period[1];
If Period < 6 then Period = 6;
If Period > 50 then Period = 50;
Period = .2*Period + .8*Period[1];
SmoothPeriod = .33*Period + .67*SmoothPeriod[1];

HH = High;
LL = Low;
For count = 0 to Int(CycPart*SmoothPeriod) -
  1 begin
      If High[count] > HH then HH = High[count];
      If Low[count] < LL then LL = Low[count];
End;
If HH - LL <> 0 then Stochastic = (Close - LL) /
  (HH - LL);

    Plot1(Stochastic, "Stoc");
End;
```

Figure 22.2. *(Continued).*

Commodity Channel Index

Refer to Figure 22.3 through discussion for EasyLanguage coding. The Commodity Channel Index (CCI) computes the average of the median price of each bar over the observation period.[2] It also computes the Mean Deviation (MD) from this average. The CCI is formed as the current deviation from the average price normalized to the MD. With a Gaussian probability distribution, 68 percent of all possible outcomes are contained within the first standard deviation from the mean. The CCI is scaled so that values above +100 are above the upper first standard deviation from the mean and values below −100 are below the lower first standard deviation from the mean. Multiplying the MD in the code by 0.015 implements this normalization. Many traders use this indicator as an overbought/oversold indicator with 100 or greater indicating that the market is overbought, and −100 or less that the market is oversold. Since the trading channel is being formed by the indicator, the obvious observation period is the same as the cycle length. Since the complete cycle period may not be the universal answer, we include a CycPart input as a modifier. This input allows you to optimize the observation period for each particular situation.

[2]Lambert, Donald R. "Commodity Channel Index." *Commodities Magazine* (October 1980): 40–41.

```
Inputs: Price((H+L)/2),
        CycPart(1);

Vars: Smooth(0),
      Detrender(0),
      I1(0),
      Q1(0),
      jI(0),
      jQ(0),
      I2(0),
      Q2(0),
      Re(0),
      Im(0),
      Period(0),
      SmoothPeriod(0),
      Length(0),
      count(0),
      MedianPrice(0),
      Avg(0),
      MD(0),
      CCI(0);

If CurrentBar > 5 then begin
    Smooth = (4*Price + 3*Price[1] + 2*Price[2] +
       Price[3]) / 10;
    Detrender = (.0962*Smooth + .5769*Smooth[2] -
       .5769*Smooth[4] - .0962*Smooth[6])*
       (.075*Period[1] + .54);

    {Compute InPhase and Quadrature components}
    Q1 = (.0962*Detrender + .5769*Detrender[2] -
       .5769*Detrender[4] - .0962*Detrender[6])*
       (.075*Period[1] + .54);
    I1 = Detrender[3];

    {Advance the phase of I1 and Q1 by 90 degrees}
    jI = (.0962*I1 + .5769*I1[2] - .5769*I1[4] -
       .0962*I1[6])*(.075*Period[1] + .54);
    jQ = (.0962*Q1 + .5769*Q1[2] - .5769*Q1[4] -
       .0962*Q1[6])*(.075*Period[1] + .54);
                                        (continued)
```

Figure 22.3.　EasyLanguage code to compute the adaptive CCI.

```
{Phasor addition for 3 bar averaging)}
I2 = I1 - jQ;
Q2 = Q1 + jI;

{Smooth the I and Q components before applying
  the discriminator}
I2 = .2*I2 + .8*I2[1];
Q2 = .2*Q2 + .8*Q2[1];

{Homodyne Discriminator}
Re = I2*I2[1] + Q2*Q2[1];
Im = I2*Q2[1] - Q2*I2[1];
Re = .2*Re + .8*Re[1];
Im = .2*Im + .8*Im[1];
If Im <> 0 and Re <> 0 then Period =
  360/ArcTangent(Im/Re);
If Period > 1.5*Period[1] then Period =
  1.5*Period[1];
If Period < .67*Period[1] then Period =
  .67*Period[1];
If Period < 6 then Period = 6;
If Period > 50 then Period = 50;
Period = .2*Period + .8*Period[1];
SmoothPeriod = .33*Period + .67*SmoothPeriod[1];

Length = IntPortion(CycPart*Period);
MedianPrice = (High + Low + Close) / 3;
Avg = 0;
For count = 0 to Length - 1 begin
      Avg = Avg + MedianPrice[count];
End;
Avg = Avg / Length;
MD = 0;
For count = 0 to Length - 1 begin
      MD = MD + AbsValue(MedianPrice[count] -
        Avg);
End;
MD = MD / Length;
If MD <> 0 then CCI = (MedianPrice - Avg) /
  (0.015*MD);

Plot1(CCI, "CCI");
End;
```

Figure 22.3. *(Continued).*

EPILOGUE: SPLASH DOWN

At Lift Off, we said our goal was to revolutionize the art of trading by introducing the concept of modern digital signal processing. I hope you agree that this has led to the development of some profoundly effective new trading tools. More important, we hope that these new trading tools have given you a new perspective on how to view the market as well as how to technically analyze it.

Rocket Science for Traders was written on several levels. At one level you have been given cookbook codes for trading systems with which you can begin trading immediately. The historical performance of these systems is on par, or exceeds, the performance of commercial systems that cost thousands of dollars. At another level you have genuinely new analysis tools, such as the Homodyne cycle period measurer, the Signal-to-Noise Indicator, the Instantaneous Trendline, the Sinewave Indicator, and more. These indicators view the market from entirely new perspectives and therefore augment your existing tools. I invite you to read the book again—perhaps more than once—and reach the highest level possible. That level constitutes a deep understanding of both the market and our analysis processes.

This book is by no means the final word on digital signal processing as it applies to trading. For example, Ehlers filters are engaged in a continuing state of research, evolution, and design. Through these efforts I hope to generate more accurate models of the market that will lead to even greater profits for traders. I encourage you to join me in this journey and boldly go where no trader has gone before. I look forward to hearing about your adventures in the market and invite you to share the new horizons you reach.

FOR MORE INFORMATION

Research is an ongoing process for me. The latest reports of my research can be found in technical papers and Power Point seminars on my Internet site *www.mesasoftware.com*.

Users of SuperCharts do not have a PowerEditor to write the EasyLanguage code I have presented. Many users of TradeStation wish to avoid the work of coding and debugging the indicators, paintbars, and systems although they have the PowerEditor. For you to maximize the utility of this book, you can purchase the EasyLanguage Archive (ELA) files for direct transfer into your trading platform. You can purchase the ELA files from my website *www.mesasoftware.com*, or by contacting me at

MESA Software
P.O. Box 1801
Goleta, CA 93116
(800) 633-6372

Good Trading!
John F. Ehlers

GLOSSARY

amplitude   Half the peak-to-peak value of the signal. This is equal to the length of the phasor.

analytic waveform   The standard waveforms with which traders are familiar, like the price history of a stock. An analytic waveform contains either positive frequencies or negative frequencies, but not both.

angular frequency   Denoted by the Greek symbol omega (ω). Angular frequency $= 2 * \pi *$ frequency.

attenuate   To make the wave amplitude smaller.

baseband   The information band of frequencies falling between zero frequency and half the sampling frequency (the Nyquist frequency).

Cycle Mode   Those times when the market data are short-term coherent. During these times, effective trading can be done by trading at the cyclic turning points using oscillator-type indicators.

decibel   Ten times the logarithm of a power ratio. Zero dB corresponds to a unity power ratio because Log(1)=0. Three dB corresponds to a power ratio of 2. The measure of –3 dB corresponds to a power ratio of 0.5. Six dB corresponds to a power ratio of 4. The measurement –6 dB corresponds to a power ratio of 0.25. Ten dB corresponds to a power ratio of 10.

detrend   The process of removing static and slowly varying components from price data, leaving the residual to be the cycle components. Detrending can be done in a variety of ways, the most simple of which is to take a momentum of the price.

direct current   Current flowing from a battery, as opposed to alternating current, which flows from wall plugs. Direct current has zero frequency. Direct current is analogous to the constant part of market price.

EasyLanguage   Computer code created by Omega Research for traders to write indicators and systems for TradeStation and SuperCharts. EasyLanguage is similar to Pascal with special keywords for trading.

Ehlers filter   A FIR filter whose coefficients are ranked by a statistic, but whose temporal location is retained. The coefficients are normalized to the sum of the coefficients to ensure unity low-frequency gain. The coefficients may be nonlinear to support rapid and sustained price movements.

Euler's Theorem   Sine and cosine can be expressed as complex exponential functions.

exponential waveform   The response of an Exponential Moving Average (EMA) to an impulse excitation. The filter output decays rapidly at first and maintains some finite output forever.

Finite Impulse Response (FIR) filter   A type of filter that provides an output only when an impulse is present within the filter window width. A Simple Moving Average (SMA) is this type of filter.

Hilbert Transform   A mathematical procedure that creates InPhase and Quadrature components as complex numbers from the analytic waveform.

Homodyne   Using the product of a signal multiplied by itself. A Homodyne Discriminator results from the multiplication of a complex signal with the complex conjugate of that signal delayed by one sample.

imaginary number   A real number located on the imaginary axis in the complex plane.

Infinite Impulse Response (IIR) filter   A type of filter that provides an output forever after having an impulse applied to the input. This is because the output involves an iterative computation using previous outputs as well as inputs. An Exponential Moving Average (EMA) is this type of filter.

InPhase component   The real part of the complex variable representation of the analytic waveform. The InPhase component is in phase with the cycle part of the data.

instantaneous phase   Computed as the arctangent of the ratio of the Quadrature component to the InPhase component.

Instantaneous Trendline   The Instantaneous Trendline is created by removing the dominant cycle signal component from the price data, with the result being that the residual is the trend component. The Instantaneous Trendline is computed by taking a simple average whose length is equal to the measured dominant cycle.

Lead Sine   An indicator line that leads the sine of the dominant cycle by 45 degrees in phase.

median filter   A filter whose output is the median value of prices contained within the filter observation window.

Nyquist frequency   Half the sampling frequency. This is the highest frequency that can be assigned to the baseband of sampled data without inducing aliasing. The Nyquist frequency for daily price data is 0.5 cycles per day (a 2-bar cycle).

Nyquist sampling criteria   The sampled data must have at least two samples per cycle of the highest information frequency.

Ohm's Law   A basic law of electronics that says that voltage is equal to the product of current time resistance.

Order Statistic (OS) filter   An OS filter is a filter that ranks the coefficients by a statistic rather than by temporal location within the filter. For example, a median filter (where the output is the median value of prices within the filter window) is an OS filter.

passband   The band of frequencies that are allowed to propagate through a filter with very little attenuation.

phasor diagram   A phasor is a two-dimensional vector whose tail is attached to the origin in a complex coordinate system. The phasor rotates with the angular frequency of the data cycle, and its length is equal to the wave amplitude.

power   Power is proportional to wave amplitude squared. Power is invariant with phase angle.

Quadrature component   Quadrature means being at right angles. The Quadrature component of the complex representation of the analytic waveform leads the InPhase component by 90 degrees.

rotational operator   The operator is $j = \sqrt{-1}$. This operator rotates a real number by 90 degrees, for example from the real axis to the imaginary axis.

sideband   An information band of frequencies heterodyned onto the sampling frequency or a harmonic of the sampling frequency.

Signal-to-Noise Ratio   For trading purposes, noise is defined as the average range from high to low of the price bars. Signal-to-Noise Ratio is the power ratio of the wave amplitude to the noise.

SineTrend Automatic Trading System   An automatic trading system that changes rules according to the determined market mode.

stopband   The band of frequencies that are rejected or heavily attenuated by a filter.

subordinate cycle   A calculation failure mode arising from rounding errors in iterative calculations.

transfer response   The characteristic of a filter. The description of the way a filter processes input data to provide the filtered output.

Trend Mode   Those times in the market when tradable cycles are not present. Trend Mode trading involves trend-following indicators, such as moving averages.

unity   Having a value of 1.

wave amplitude   Half the peak-to-peak value of the signal. This is equal to the length of the phasor.

zero frequency   The cycle period is infinitely long. Direct current has zero frequency.

Z Transform   A tool for algebraic solution of discrete system problems.

INDEX

A

Aliasing, 3
Alpha-Beta filter, 169
Amplitude, 241
Analog signal versus digital signal, 2
Analog transfer function (converting into digital transfer function), 138–141
Analytic signal:
  InPhase (cosine) component, 53, 54, 59
  Quadrature (sine) component, 54, 59
Analytic waveform, 47, 241
Angular frequency, 46, 241
Attenuate, 241
Automatic trading systems
  SineTrend Automatic Trading System, 119–130
  ZeroLag Intraday Trading System, 170–175
Averaging, 17

B

Baseband, 241
Bel (compared with decibel), 5
Bessel functions:
  Hankel Transforms and, 131
  Meijer Transforms and, 131
Bicycle diagram, 48, 49
Butterworth filter, 153, 155
Butterworth filter tables, 156, 157

C

CD (Closes Down), 228, 229
Coherent waveshapes, 5
Commodity Channel Index, 235
Complex addition, 43–44
Complex numbers:
  defined, 42
  Euler's Theorem, 46
  expressed in exponential form, 44–47
  expressed in polar coordinates, 44
Complex plane, 43
Complex signals, 53
Complex variables, 41–49
Continuous systems:
  Fourier Transforms and, 135
  Laplace Transforms and, 135
Cosine functions, 46
CU (Closes Up), 228–229
Cutoff frequency, 6
Cycle measurement comparison, 73–77
Cycle mode, 12, 14, 15, 21, 35, 60, 107, 108, 113, 119, 130, 206, 241
Cycle mode rules and criteria, 113, 119
Cycle period measurement, 63–77
  Dual Differentiator technique, 70, 72, 73
  Homodyne Discriminator technique, 67, 69, 70
  Phase Accumulation technique, 63, 64, 66

Cyclic turning points in market (phasor diagrams), 215–225
Cylindrical coordinates:
Legendre Transforms and, 131
Mellin Transforms and, 131

D
Decibel, 5, 241
Detrend, 241
Detrending filter, 37
Differential equation problems:
Laplace Transform and, 132–134
Transform arithmetic and, 141
Diffusion equation, 11, 12, 14, 17
Digital signal, 2
Digital signal processing, 2
Digital signal versus analog
signal, 2
Discrete time signal, 2, 3
Distance coefficient Ehlers filter,
193, 194
Dominant cycle amplitude, 59
Dominant cycle period, 59
Dominant cycle phase, 59
Drunkard's Walk problem, 11, 15,
107, 113, 203
Dual Differentiator technique of
cycle period measurement, 70,
73
Dynamic Linked Library (DLL), 152

E
EasyLanguage, 6–7, 152, 242
EasyLanguage code
for computing adaptive CCI,
236–237
for computing adaptive RSI,
230–231
for computing adaptive Stochastic,
233–234
for computing distance coefficient
Ehlers filter, 193
for computing dominant cycle
phase, 96–99
for computing Ehlers filter, 189

for computing Hilbert Oscillator,
90–92
for computing Instantaneous
Trendline, 108–110
for computing MESA Adaptive
Moving Average (MAMA),
181–183
for computing Optimum Predictor,
208–210
for computing predictive filters,
209–210
for computing signal-to-noise ratio,
80–82
for computing SineTrend Automatic Trading System,
120–123
for computing Sinewave Indicator,
100–103
for computing ZeroLag Intraday
Trading System, 171–175
for creating ASCII file of InPhase
and Quadrature data, 216, 217
for identifying market mode,
114–117
Efficiency ratio, 178
Ehlers, John, 119
Ehlers filter, 185–195
characteristics of, 187
EasyLanguage code for, 189
flexibility and adaptability, 191
formulation, 187–188
performance, 190
statistic, 188
term defined, 242
Euler's equations, 53
Euler's Theorem, 46, 242
Exponential Moving Average (EMA),
27–31, 167–170
characteristics of, 32
computing alpha term, 29
as example of IIR filter, 166, 185
in Kalman filtering, 167–170
noise as, 80
Optimum Predictive Filter and,
205–206

recursive factor, 27
response to step function, 28–29
Exponential waveform, 242

F
Fast Fourier Transform (FFT) tool, 197
constraints, 197–198
unsuitability for market analysis, 197
Finite Impulse Response (FIR) filter, 143–150
coefficient, 143
definition, 243
examples of, 143
impulse response, 143
lag, 144, 150
Following Adaptive Moving Average (FAMA), 181
Fourier series, 54
Fourier theory, 3
Fourier Transform, 23, 24, 55, 134
continuous systems and, 135
parallels with Z Transform, 135
steady-state analysis and, 134

G
Gauss, Karl Friedrich, 17
Gaussian distribution, 17
Gaussian filters, 156, 158–162
Gaussian filter tables, 162–165
Group delay, 158

H
Hankel Transform, 131
Heterodyning, 3, 51
Hilbert Oscillator, 92
Hilbert Transform, 51–62, 79, 95, 215, 242
Hilbert Transformer, 54–58, 60, 67, 206, 207
improving amplitude response, 57
minimizing lag, 58
Homodyne Discriminator, 228

Homodyne Discriminator method of cycle period measurement, 67, 69, 70
Homodyning, 242

I
Imaginary numbers, 42–44, 49
Improved Hilbert Transformer, 57–58
Impulse, 34
Impulse invariant analog/digital conversion method, 138–141
Induced lag, 17
Infinite Impulse Response (IIR) filters, 151–165
accuracy considerations, 152
described, 242
limit cycles, 152
rounding errors, 152
scaling considerations, 152
transfer response, 151
InPhase component, 54, 56, 59–61, 63, 64, 66, 67, 69, 70, 72, 77, 79, 80, 216, 242
Instantaneous phase, 242
Instantaneous Trendline, 22, 23, 59, 107–112, 242
Intraday trade, 170
Inverse Laplace Transform, 138

J
Jerk, 34

K
Kalman, R. E., 167
Kalman filtering, 167
Kaufman, Perry, 178
Kaufman's Adaptive Moving Average (KAMA), 177–179

L
Lag, 17–19, 31, 64, 95, 158, 159
Lag (removing), 167–176
Lane, Dr. George, 232

Laplace Transform
   continuous systems and, 135
   differential equations and,
      132–134
   transient conditions in electrical
      circuits and, 132–134
Lead Sine, 243
Legendre Transform, 131
Linear filters, 185
Lower sideband, 52
Low-pass filters, 158

M
Market analysis (measuring market
      spectra), 197–203
Market cycle, 47
Market efficiency hypothesis, 9
Market mode identification:
   Cycle mode criteria, 113
   Trend mode criteria, 113–114
Market modes, 9–15
Mean Deviation (MD), 235
Median filter:
   characteristics, 186
   defined, 243
Meijer Transform, 131
Mellin Transform, 131
MESA Adaptive Moving Average
      (MAMA), 179–181
MESA spectrum measurement tech-
      nique, 198, 200–203
Momentum
   defined, 35
   as a detrending filter, 37
   and sine wave, 35
Momentum functions, 33–40
Moving averages, 17–32
   characteristics of, 17, 32
   Exponential Moving Average
      (EMA), 27–31
   induced lag, 17
   predictive moving averages, 212
   purpose of, 31
   Simple Moving Average (SMA),
      18–25

Weighted Moving Average (WMA),
      25–27
Multipole filter, 153

N
Negative frequency, 51
Negative numbers (as mathematical
      concept), 41
*New Concepts in Technical Trading
      Systems* (Wilder), 228
New Technical Trader, The (Chande
      and Kroll), 179
Noise, 79, 80, 83, 93
Nonlinear filters, 185
Normal distribution, 17
Nyquist frequency, 3, 243
Nyquist sampling criteria, 52, 243
Nyquist sampling theorem, 3

O
Ohm's Law, 243
Optimized Stochastic Indicator, 232
Optimum estimation (concept), 167
Optimum Predictive Filters, 205–213
   conditions for validity, 206
   defined, 205–206
   Exponential Moving Average
      (EMA) and, 205–206
   overview, 205
Optimum Predictor, 208–211
Order Statistic (OS) filters, 186, 243
Orthogonal numbers, 43

P
Pascal computer language, 6
Passband, 243
Periodic impulse train, 3
Phase Accumulation technique of
      cycle period measurement,
      63–64, 66
Phase shift, 21
Phasor diagrams
   for anticipating cyclic turning
      points in market, 215–225
   defined, 243

dominant cycle, 48–49
secondary cycle, 48–49
for Sinewave Indicator, 100
Poisson probability distribution, 206
Pole, 152
Power, 243
Predictive filters, 205–213

Q
Quadrature, 54
Quadrature component, 54, 56,
59–61, 63, 64, 66, 67, 69, 70, 72,
77, 79, 80, 216, 243

R
Ramp function, 33–34
Random Walk Model, 10–11
*Random Walks: Theory and Selected
Applications* (Weiss and Rubin),
10
Real numbers, 42–44, 49
Redmont, Rick, 229
Relative phases, 49
Relative Strength Indicator (RSI),
1–2, 228–229
Removing lag, 167–176
Rotating phasor, 49
Rotational operator (defined), 243–244
Rubin, R. J., 10

S
Sampled data, 131
Sampling frequency, 51, 52
Sideband, 244
Signal amplitude, 47, 79, 80
Signal-to-noise ratio, 59, 79–89, 244
Signal-to-noise-ratio computation,
80–83
Signal-to-noise-ratio computation
(alternate method), 83, 86–88
Simple Moving Average (SMA), 18–25
attenuation, 24–25
characteristics of, 32
as example of FIR filter, 143, 145,
150, 185

instantaneous trendline, 22–23
lag, 19–20
momentum of, 39–40
phase shift, 21–22
static lag, 18–21
Sine functions, 46
SineTrend Automatic Trading System, 119–130
applied to Deutschemark futures,
128
applied to Treasury bond futures,
119–130
EasyLanguage code for, 120–123
performance after optimizing
instantaneous trendline, 125,
127, 128
performance using complete
system, 124
performance using cycle mode
only, 124
performance using trend mode
only, 124
Sinewave Indicator, 59, 95–105
advantages as a cycle mode predictive indicator, 100
EasyLanguage code for,
100–103
Slater, Tim, 229
Smoothing, 17, 19, 20, 26, 31
S&P futures, 170–175
Spherical coordinates:
Legendre Transforms and, 131
Mellin Transforms and, 131
Statistical Theory of Communication (Lee), 206
Stochastic Indicator, 229, 232
Stopband, 244
Suboptimal filters, 168
Subordinate cycle, 244

T
Telegrapher's Equation, 11–12, 14
*Theory and Application of Digital
Signal Processing* (Rabiner and
Gold), 54

Trading Systems and Methods (Kaufman), 178, 197
Transfer response, 244
Transform arithmetic, 131–141
Transforms:
 Fourier Transform, 134
 Hankel Transform, 131
 Laplace Transform, 132–134
 Legendre Transform, 131
 Meijer Transform, 131
 Mellin Transform, 131
 Z Transform, 131, 135–138
Transient analysis, 132–134
Treasury bonds futures contract, 119, 124, 125, 127
Trend mode, 12, 14, 15, 107, 108, 113, 119, 130, 207, 244
Trend mode rules and criteria, 113–114, 119
Trends, 107–112
Trigonometric identities, 53

U
Unity, 244
Upper sideband, 52

V
Variable Index Dynamic Average (VIDYA), 179
Volatility, 179

W
Wave amplitude, 244
Weighted Moving Average (WMA), 25–27
 characteristics of, 32
 compared with Simple Moving Average, 25
 as example of FIR filter, 144
 reduced lag, 26–27
Whiffles, 49
Wiener-Hopf equation, 206
Wilder, Welles, 227

Z
ZEMA (zero-lag EMA), 169–170
Zero (as mathematical concept), 41
Zero frequency, 244
Zero frequency harmonic, 52
ZeroLag Exponential Moving Average, 170
ZeroLag Instantaneous Trendline, 170
ZeroLag Intraday Trading System:
 EasyLanguage code for, 172–175
 trading rules, 171, 175
Z Transform:
 defined, 244
 discrete systems and, 135–138
 parallels with Fourier Transform, 135
 sampled data and, 131